To: _____

From: _____

Date: _____

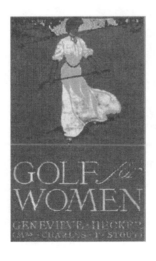

Honoring Golf's Literary Tradition

*Legacy Golf is dedicated to the celebration of golf's earliest
literary gems. In reissuing these landmark instructional and
historical works, Legacy Golf hopes to enhance the reader's
appreciation and passion for the game. Those interested
in learning more about the history of golf should contact
Golf House, the United States Golf Association's Museum
and Library, located in Far Hills, NJ, or visit
its web site at www.usga.org.*

www.legacy-golf.com

Legacy Golf is an imprint of St. Remy Media, Inc.
Maison Bagg, 682 William Street, Montreal, Quebec H3C 1N9

Published in association with the literary agency of Alive Communications, Inc.,
7680 Goddard St., Suite 200, Colorado Springs, CO 80920

To contact Wally Armstrong, write or call:
Gator Golf Enterprises, Inc.
P.O. Box 941911, Maitland, FL 32794
(407) 644-3398   e-mail: snagwally@cfl.rr.com

National Library of Canada Cataloguing in Publication Data
Hecker, Genevieve, 1884-1960.
    Golf for women

Reprint. Originally published: New York : Baker & Taylor, 1904.

ISBN 1-894827-01-5

    1. Golf for women. I. Title.

GV966.H32 2001   796.352'082   C2001-902839-3

Foreword

I started playing golf in 1939 at the Findlay Country Club in my home town of Findlay, Ohio. With much hard practice and some instruction from the pro Leonard Schmutte (at a cost of 50 cents per lesson), I fell in love with the game. I remember fondly those early days, the men dressed as dapper as any in the world and the women in their long skirts. Since that time, golf has been my passion. Reading *Golf for Women*, I knew that its author, Genevieve Hecker, shared my passion. Her remarkable book is the first ever written specifically for women. As such, it has become a foundation of women's golf instruction in this country. Amazingly, it was originally published in 1904, when she was just 21 years old.

Hecker was a great player and her talent is evident in the pages of this book. Although some of her instruction on the golf swing is quite different from what is being taught today, it was accurate in its time. Remember that soft, hickory-shafted clubs were the norm and restrictive clothing was worn by all women golfers. (Hecker suggests a full-length, broadcloth, tailor-made skirt in any color but white as the best golfing outfit, and mentions that many of the older ladies would be wearing corsets!) The key to success was to generate a long, flowing swing, with the focus on good timing and rhythm. Hecker's swing-sequence photos reveal just such a swing. As far as the psychological side of the game is concerned, her instruction is as valid today as it was when it was written. She offers a wealth of practical, no-nonsense advice concerning practice and on-course strategy, etiquette, and the mental game. This sometimes humorous and always insightful information will help anyone who reads it today.

Beyond its value as an instructional tool, however, is the great impact this book had on women's golf in a day when women were not welcomed on many courses. By writing *Golf for Women*, young Genevieve Hecker lit a spark in women, encouraging them to play the game, and showing them how to play it well. Today the book serves as a testament to the long history of women's golf in this country. As someone who has devoted a good deal of my life to advancing women's golf and women's golf instruction, I'm happy to add this work to my collection. Once you've read it, you'll feel the same way.

Peggy Kirk Bell

Introduction

As a golf teacher and someone fascinated by the history of the game, I am thrilled to be a part of the reissuing of *Golf for Women*. The first book on women's golf in America, it is an incredibly complete instructional resource and a unique portrait of the game's early days in this country. This republication also gives me a chance to introduce you to one of golf's most amazing yet least known characters, the book's author, Genevieve Hecker.

It is not everyday one comes upon such an an intriguing character as Hecker. In my many years of reading about and exploring the history of golf, I have happened on a few. But none has captured my imagination as she has. She was a fantastic player, a dynamic personality, and on top of that, an incredible writer and philosopher of the game. She was also a woman of great beauty. Amazingly, at the time of publication of this book, she was only 21. For accomplishments at a young age, Hecker could certainly give Tiger Woods a run for his money!

Where did she come from? Well, we know she was raised on the Wee Burn Golf Club in Noroton, Connecticut. A six-hole layout on the site of what is now a high school, it was the first course in the state. The club was founded in 1896 and charged a membership fee of $125 and annual dues of $25, both significant amounts of money at that time. George Strath served as both course architect and golf pro, and it was he who somehow brought Hecker to such proficiency in such a short time. Though the fees at Wee Burn were high, the course was not without its peculiarities. For one, the leaseholder of the property, a Mr. Strangward, insisted that nothing should interfere with his use of the course for grazing his cattle. The fourth hole was fenced off for the cows and special rules were put in place in case the "hazard" came into play.

Just 14 when she took up the game, Hecker rose to prominence quickly. By 1900 she had won three club championships and one regional title, the Women's Metropolitan Golf Association championship. The following year, she won the first of two consecutive U.S. Women's Amateur championships. With her victories, Hecker assumed a prominent role in the women's golf scene of the day. It was a very decorous world, with women dressed in skirts and often wearing wide-brimmed hats. With her incredible talent and beauty, Hecker took it by storm.

By all accounts, she was in a different category than the other women players of the day. Her long, smooth swing and seemingly effortless power produced drives up to 200 yards long, revolutionary for the time. Her scores, including a women's record 86 at Baltusrol in 1905, often rivalled those of the country's best male golfers. Hecker's rare abilities, combined with her cool, relaxed style and youthful beauty, captivated fans and journalists everywhere she played.

The day's golf writers gushed over her talents. In a *Book of Sport*, 1901, she is described as exhibiting "the most brilliant and perfect game ever played by a woman in America." The magazine *Ladies Golf* in 1904 referred to her as "a wonder," and for her long game judged her to be "in a class by herself." Another story of the day described her play at the 1902 U.S. Women's Amateur championship in these glowing terms: "It is conceded that while sometime there may arise a woman golfer who will defeat her, there never will be one who will play in more ideal style." Golfing fans were completely smitten. At the championship in 1902, a crowd of 3,000 admirers followed her for the first two rounds. Genevieve Hecker was America's first full-blown women's golfing sensation.

What you'll find out reading *Golf for Women* is that she was also one of the game's most knowledgeable students. The chapters of this book, which originally appeared in the magazine *Golf*, contain information on all parts of the game "to the feminine inquiring mind and from a woman's standpoint." And it is amazingly complete. Hecker addresses virtually every aspect of the game, from etiquette to equipment to golf course lengths for women to competitive strategies in medal and match play. She offers sections on the short game and psychology, along with many practice drills to aid in perfecting golf skills. She also talks about the causes of poor shots, the best way to play in the wind, and what to do when you are over-golfed. And she includes an early description of the yips that matches any other I have read.

With *Golf for Women*, 21-year-old Genevieve Hecker produced an instructional masterwork. But more than that, she gave us, the players of today, a valuable tool to learn about the early stages of women's golf in this country. For that, she deserves to be remembered. Thanks to this book, she will be for a very long time.

Wally Armstrong

Opinions of the Day

"We have read many dissertations on golf, but this is the first petticoat golf that has come to our attention. Miss Hecker uses but few technical terms and handles her subject in as masterly a manner as she does her clubs."
—*The Independent*, New York, NY, June 23, 1904

"It would be hard to find a more helpful, timely and suggestive book for women golfers than this latest addition to golfing literature."
—*Country Life in America*, New York, NY, August 1, 1904

"At present, when golf has become one of the recognized fields for feminine endeavor, the value and timeliness of the present book are clearly apparent."
—*Public Opinion*, New York, NY, May 12, 1904

"Well indeed does our author grasp the feminine requirements and meet them."
—*The Los Angeles Times*, Los Angeles, CA, April 10, 1904

And from Miss Hecker herself upon publication of her book:
"No matter how valuable to a man the present text-books of the game may be, I have found by my own personal experience, and that of many of my friends, that there were many points about the best of them which were, perhaps, familiar as A, B, C's to a man, but wholly incomprehensible to a woman. That this is quite to be expected is natural, for how can a man understand the ways and moods and means which must be taken into consideration when a woman prepares to golf?"

Golf *for* Women

By

GENEVIEVE HECKER
(Mrs. Charles T. Stout)

*National Woman Champion 1901-02 and 1902-03;
Did Not Compete 1903-04; Champion of
Women's Metropolitan Association
in 1900-01 and 1901-02*

With a Chapter by

RHONA K. ADAIR
*Three Years English Open Champion and Five Years
Irish Open Champion*

New York: THE BAKER & TAYLOR COMPANY
33-37 East Seventeenth Street, Union Square, North

CONTENTS

ILLUSTRATIONS

7

PUBLISHERS' NOTE

The publishers of this volume beg to acknowledge the courtesy of Messrs. Harper & Brothers, publishers of "Golf," in permitting a reproduction of the chapters of this book and the photographs, which originally appeared in that magazine.

GOLF FOR WOMEN

CHAPTER I

INTRODUCTORY

ALTHOUGH there have been in the past few years a great many books written upon golf, detailing how to play the game, and the things one should do and likewise leave undone, there has never been a book which presented the Royal and Ancient game to the feminine inquiring mind and from a woman's standpoint. It is my purpose and desire to supply this deficiency, so far as I may be able to do so, in the chapters that shall make up this book.

No matter how valuable to a man the present text-books of the game may be, I have found by my own personal experience and that of many of my friends that there were many points about the best of them which were, perhaps, familiar as the A B C's to a man, but wholly incomprehensible to a woman.

That this is quite to be expected is natural, for how can a man understand the ways and moods and means which must be taken into consideration when a woman prepares to golf?

Until quite recently—that is to say, the last six or seven years—women's place in golf has been so comparatively unimportant that no woman has felt it incumbent upon her to blaze the path, as it were, for her faltering yet enthusiastic sisters. Happily, that time has now gone, and it has gone never to return. Women in England and Scotland, as well as in America, but particularly here, have taken up the game with so much enthusiasm—have become such " cranks," to quote from the slang of the day—and, better than all, have become so thoroughly alive to its benefits from a purely physical standpoint, that it does not seem as though it would ever be allowed to drop into the oblivion which has heretofore followed all the sports which have in turn been the fad of the hour.

Nor is woman's place in golf secured to her only by the sufferance and good-nature of her masculine relatives. When she appears on a links the flutter of her skirt is not the signal for a deep and heart-felt, albeit suppressed, burst of profanity, even from those devotees who consider that the old Scotchman who said, " Never, my boys, allow business to interfere with golf," uttered one of the greatest sayings of the world.

It is quite true that the Powers that Be at St. Andrews, Scotland, by a majority of one, refused recently to allow the Woman's national championship to be played there, but such a storm of indignation arose over this action, in both the ranks of the club and among the towns-people, all of whom under various rules and restrictions use the historic old course, that the committee have

practically decided to recall their decision,
and most humbly invite the ladies to
use their links, and, if they like, their clubs
 nd everything that is theirs, for the championship meeting, and as long after as they
please. Such is woman's delightful position
across the water, and here it is even more firm.

When women in America first began to play
golf, they were allowed at many of the big
clubs to use the links only at certain hours on
certain days when it was thought that their
presence would not incommode the Lords of
Creation.

The idea that a woman could learn to play
a really good and serious game of golf was
laughed to scorn, and if there were many women who evinced a desire to play at the various clubs, numbers of them would doubtless
have followed the example of the Shinnecock
Hills Club and laid out a course exclusively
for women.

The small number who, at its first introduction, took up the game, however, made

this quite unnecessary; so, at least, it was thought.

The first courses laid out in America were very short, and consequently easy. That of the Morris County Club, one of the finest in the country then, as now, had in those days but seven holes, and not one of them was over a drive and iron-shot in length. The women were therefore able to reach them with a drive and brassey, and so were as well off as the men, and their scores soon began to compare very favorably with those of their masculine competitors. This was also true of other courses and clubs, and the women naturally asked for the privilege of playing at any and all hours, urging as an excuse their ability to make low scores.

After much hesitation and head-shaking on the part of those men who, never having had sisters, had no idea of the physical capabilities of a girl, and her ability to do anything she really wanted to, permission was granted —reluctantly, it must be confessed, but nev-

ertheless granted—to them except on Satur-
day afternoons, when the course was sure to
be overcrowded by masculine golfers.

The women took their hardly won permission with joy, and proceeded to demonstrate
that they could play good golf by taking on
their detractors for a round and soundly beat-
ing them. From that day women have had an
undisputed place on the links, and for the
past three or four years it has been esteemed
an honor for even the Amateur champion to
be asked to play in a mixed foursome by
any one of a dozen of our leading women
players.

As an evidence of how steadily and impress-
ively the quality of golf which our women are
playing is improving, the action on July 1,
1902, of the Shinnecock Hills Golf Club, one
of the oldest, finest, and most conservative
clubs in America, of giving up the maintenance
of its women's links, speaks volumes. This is
only one instance, but it shows the tendency.

Another point which shows clearly how

women are improving in their standard of play is the fact that it is not now customary to shorten the men's course for a woman's tournament—even when the drives from the tee require a carry of from 100 to 120 yards, and the bunkers placed to catch a poor second shot are proportionately far away.

Still another and a most convincing argument, were it needed, to prove the advance in woman's skill, is the fact that with hardly an exception the women who were the stars of the country four or five years ago are hardly rated as being in the second class now, although they are invariably playing as well as, and in most cases better than they were, when at the zenith of their fame. Nor is it in any one or two particular points in which the woman of to-day excels those of a few years ago. It is in every department of the game. She drives a much longer ball, she plays her brassey and iron-shots better, and she lays her approaches closer to the hole. If her putting has not gained in the improvement to the same extent as have the other departments of her play, it has held its own at least. For these facts there are two reasons accountable. One is that with the spread of the game the number of first-class players is, of course, increased. For instance, if there is one in every 1000, in every 10,000 there are ten, and if this ratio is carried out to a ten times greater degree, these 100 players form a large enough number to affect the percentage of good players materially; the other reason lies in the age at which the women who are prominent today began to golf.

Before proceeding further, however, I wish to most emphatically emphasize the fact that there is no royal road to success in golf. It comes only by the hardest kind of assiduous and thoughtful practice.

Furthermore, the practice must be done in the proper way.

Great achievements can be accomplished only when they are attempted in the orthodox style, and to acquire the proper swing should be the first and most lasting ambition of every woman who sets out to master the sport.

If she does not master it, her efforts to improve will all be in vain, and no matter how brilliantly she may play for a single round by means of some unorthodox trick of style, it will surely prove but a delusion and a snare in the end.

To play golf of the championship class, it is essential that a woman start to learn the game before she is thirty years old, and each year she begins before that, after reaching her fourteenth birthday, is just that much in her favor. It is true that we have in this country a number of women who have obtained national prominence as golfers who did not begin to play until they were thirty years or more of age, but it has also been conclusively proven by the records of the game that the number of these women is becoming smaller each year, and a study of their style of play demonstrates that they have not the power to execute the strokes of the game requiring the utmost freedom of movement with anything like the ability which their younger and more lissome sisters possess.

To judge from the style of play adopted by the best examples of this class of women golfers, it will be found that their lack of early training lies more particularly in their driving and brassey play, although all shots requiring a full stroke are more or less affected. None of them have ever acquired a full swing, their club under no circumstances ever describing more than a three-quarter circle, and usually not going back further than does the club in the " baseball " swing, which men like Mr. H. P. Toler and Mr. J. A. Tyng have made famous, and which is really hardly more than a half-stroke.

This is also the stroke of nearly every other woman who has taken up golf at the age of thirty or more, and while it may be due in part to the fact that women of that age are much more apt to wear corsets and tight clothes generally than are the girls in their teens, it must be admitted that age has something to do with it. The traditions of all other lines of sport hold that no one ever became really great who had not begun his career at an early age, and golfing traditions hold more strenuously than do those of any other sport to this axiom. In fact, there has been for many years a story told at old St. Andrews which illustrates this point to a nicety.

A beginner was anxiously inquiring of a dour plain-spoken old professional how long it took a man to become a great golfer. " Well," said the old fellow slowly, " if your father and your grandfather and his father before him were muckle good golfers, and you began as a little child, by the time you were grown up you should play pretty fair."

That may have been true for England and Scotland, but in America our men and women have disproved it by the way in which they have in two or three or four years reached the championship class; and this class in America is, I am convinced, very little behind the front rank of players across the sea.

Nor have we failed to produce feminine players whose game has been a refutation of the tradition that it is necessary to begin young. It is true that there is no such encouraging example to the portly matrons and elderly maids in the ranks of their own sex as the men have in our present Amateur national champion, Mr. Walter J. Travis, a man who was quite, if not considerably past, thirty years of age when he began to play golf. It is said by many good judges that he has reached the limit of his play, and that he cannot improve further, but this was said of him in 1899, when he disproved it most conclusively by his wonderful series of victories and the increased length of his long game in 1900. In his style there was little improvement to be noticed, but he did lengthen his swing a little, which shows that a man beginning even as late in life as he did can still acquire good form.

It is this fact more than any other which makes one feel convinced that it is more the fault of their clothes than their years which is the trouble with our more elderly women in their efforts to acquire the best style.

Summing up this matter of age, I think that it is much better for a woman to begin to golf at sixteen years old, but she need not despair of becoming a really first-class player even though she has arrived at the age of thirty without knowing the difference between a brassey and a hazard, while she can rest assured that so long as she is young enough to walk around the links and raise her arms with a club in her grasp as high as her head, she can learn to become a golfer.

PHYSICAL QUALIFICATIONS

As I have said before, there is no royal road to success in golf; and good physique, although it may aid one who has the correct principles to get the most out of the game, will not in itself enable one to play well.

Neither can it be said that the most successful golfers are either big or little. Mr. Herbert Harriman, the Amateur champion of 1900, is a big, broad-shouldered man, who stands six feet at least, and weighs probably 200 pounds, while Mr. Walter J. Travis, the present title-holder, is by no means a tall man, and tips the scales at probably less than 150 pounds.

James Braid, the man who last year defeated Vardon and Taylor for the English Open championship, is six feet four inches tall, but not as broad in proportion. He is probably the longest average driver in the world, for he recently averaged in an eighteen-hole round drives of 243 yards.

Of the extremes in women who have become famous, perhaps the most notable is Miss Beatrix Hoyt, who held the Woman's national championship for three years in succession. She is about five feet two inches tall, and is very slight, while Miss Cassatt of Philadelphia, and a well-known figure in

national tournaments, is within an inch or
two of six feet, and is very well propor-
tioned.

Thus it may be seen that no one, large or
small, or medium-sized, is barred from becoming a championship possibility by the limitations of her physique.

The whole question resolves itself into acquiring the proper style, as I have heretofore
emphasized.

Several women who perhaps have made up
in other sports for lack of skill by a super-
abundance of muscle have said to me that they
disagreed with me in the statement that one
need not be especially strong in order to play
class golf, and that by all the laws of common-sense the stronger person would play
the better through having the greater
power.

This is quite true provided each has the
same amount of skill, but if my critics had
seen, as I have, a man who, in his day, was
considered one of the greatest athletes Yale

ever turned out, a football guard, crew and track man, outdriven by a twelve-year-old boy, they might feel inclined to think less highly of pure muscle. The reason was that the boy knew how to do it, while the ex-Yale giant relied on his strength alone.

When I say a person's size has no effect on the game he may develop I do not include in the statement any enormously stout person, or people who are in any way out of the ordinary, but only those of nearly average proportions.

THE QUESTION OF CLOTHES

The most common dress for the links among women is a shirt-waist and short skirt. The material for each may be whatsoever the wearer chooses, the predominating idea being to select something comfortable and light enough not to tire one in the tramp over the course. Most women vary their golfing clothes with the season of the year, just as they do their street and afternoon gowns, but this is by no means necessary.

The most popular style of costume during the summer months is a cotton shirt-waist with a short skirt of white duck or piqué, but personally I do not like this color, because I have found it has a tendency to make me take my eye off the ball, particularly in putting, and for this reason I think a broadcloth, tailor-made skirt of any other color than white is the best to play in.

The matter of shoes may also be left to the individual taste of the player. Some prefer high-laced boots of heavy calf-skin, because of the support which they give to the ankles. Others, equally good players, wear nothing but low shoes. In any case they should be of at least medium weight with broad, comfortable soles and low military heels.

No one can play good golf without a secure stance, and the shoes, consequently, should be non-slippable.

Many players trust their footing to rubber soles. These are very good in dry weather, but useless in wet, and it is a bad plan, I think, to change frequently, just as a constant change of clubs tends to unsettle one's play.

I think the best all-round shoe, therefore, is one with hobnails in the sole. This is the kind that I wear, although I use rubber heels instead of leather ones with hobnails, because the weight in making a stroke is rested rather on the sole of the foot than the heel, which makes it necessary to have the former particularly secure, while the rubber heels tire one much less in walking than do the ordinary kind.

I also make a point of having my shoes heavy, and have them made with a double sole, because I think they are much less apt to hurt one's feet than are light ones in tramping over the rough ground sometimes found on golf courses.

The question of whether or not to wear a hat is another point in which the individual taste of the player can have full sway. Some players wear hats, and others do not. Still others do one day and do not another.

I am one of the latter division, and I do not think it has the slightest influence on one's game. If the eyes are not very strong and affected at all by the glare of the summer sun, a hat with a good broad brim that will act as a shade will be found a relief.

I do not personally like to play golf in gloves, unless my hands are a little sore, and I think that the best players, both here and in England, agree with me unanimously on this point. Certainly none of the professionals play in gloves, and, after all, for grand golf day after day and week after week the professionals are a long way ahead of the amateur, even though the latter occasionally strikes a gait which is equal to the " pro.'s " best. Great delicacy of touch is needed to play a golf stroke to perfection, and it stands to reason that one can obtain this much more truly with the bare hand than if the sense of contact must be transmitted through a heavy glove.

Another point against the glove is that the club is much more apt to slip in one's hand, and this follows especially in cold weather, and no matter how much pitch is put on it.

The question of corsets is one which a woman can decide for herself. In the days of tight lacing they were out of the question, but now that common-sense governs their use, they play no more important part in determining good golf than does the weight or color of a player's skirt.

TECHNICAL TERMS

The game of golf is so utterly unlike any other, that no matter how well versed one may be in other sports, a knowledge of them will be of no use to the novice in golf, either as an aid to a correct understanding of the principles of the game, or to the proper method of play.

There are so many technical terms which are necessary to express one's meaning when talking about golf that it has a vocabulary of its own, and it is impossible to write or talk about the game without using many of these terms.

The names of the clubs, for example, convey no meaning at all from their sound, except, perhaps, the " driver " and " putter." The first would naturally be supposed to be the club with which the drives are made, but everyone does not know that the drive is the first shot in the playing of each hole. The fact that there are two meanings to the word " tee " also has a confusing effect on the mind of the novice, and indeed many who would be indignant at being put in this category. Primarily it is the space of ground from which the player makes her first shot at each hole, but it also means the little pat or mound of sand upon which she places her ball for this shot.

The most useful word in the golfer's vocabulary—or at least the one which will describe the golfer's efforts at first, most fre-

quently, I am afraid—is, " foozle," which
can be applied to any stroke which does not
result the way the player intended it to
do.

A " hazard " is any difficulty, natural or
artificial, and a " cop-bunker " is a mound of
earth over which the ball must be played to
reach the hole. It should have a sand trench
three or four feet wide in front of its face, and
occasionally the trench is also placed on the
other side as well. Shallow, sandy pits are
known as " pot-bunkers " or " traps," and in
general any piece of waste sandy ground is a
" bunker."

All bunkers are hazards, but all hazards
are not bunkers by any means, a fact which
many even fairly proficient golfers are either
unaware of or ignore.

To " slice " is to drive the ball in a curve to
the right, and a " pull " is for it to come to the
left.

A " sclaff " is hitting the ground before
or at the same time as one hits the ball, so

that the stroke loses something of its force, and the opposite extreme is appropriately called a "top." Another appropriately coined term is "addressing the ball," and it describes the attempt of the player to settle into a satisfactory position for making the shot.

The "caddie" is the person who condescends to carry one's clubs in the round, and the "cup" is merely another name for the hole.

The "follow-through" is that part of the stroke which is made after the club has come in contact with the ball, and no essential of style is more important. "Approaching" is any stroke calculated to place the ball on the putting-green, be it made with driver, brassey, or anything else, except a shot made from the tee, which is always a drive. When the "green" is spoken of, it is the putting-green that is meant, and this is the space within a radius of twenty yards from the hole, exclusive of hazards.

The " fair-green " is properly that part of the course which lies between the several tees and their corresponding putting-greens.

An " iron " is any club with an iron head, and the " links " is another general term for the ground on which the game is played. There is no such word as " link " to designate a single hole.

The " long-game " is any full shot, and the " short-game " conversely means any stroke played with less than a full swing.

The " odd " is one stroke more than the opponent has played, and the " like " an equal number. " To press " is to endeavor to hit the ball harder than usual, in order to gain greater distance. " Putting " is the art of getting the ball into the hole, once it has reached the green.

With these startling additions to one's former vocabulary safely and surely in mind, the novice should now learn a few of women's most common faults in order that she may herself avoid them.

FEMININE FAILINGS IN PARTICULAR

This is a topic on which it is more than
unusually hard to generalize, for just as
golfer's have their pet club and certain strokes
which they must play unusually well, so also
have they certain idiosyncrasies which crop
out to their undoing time after time, despite
their utmost efforts to remedy the fault.

This can be accomplished, of course, with
time and patience after the trouble is located,
but oftentimes it will take many weeks to discover just what is the trouble, and in trying
one new thing after another, hoping to cure
some particular fault, another equally as disastrous may be developed.

Naturally, this is discouraging, but in learning the cause and effect of shots as thoroughly
as one must in studying out the cause of bad
play, one will acquire a fund of invaluable
knowledge if one wishes to become a really
great player.

Perhaps the greatest fault among women

is impatience. They are so anxious to make
their shot that many and many a time they
step up to the ball and play it with no more
than a casual glance at its lie, the distance to
be covered, and the nature of the shot which
will yield the best results. I have often seen
women, even among the best players, play a
full shot with a brassey or driver, simply because they had it in their hand, when, if they
had looked at the distance for a fraction of a
second, they would have realized that a
mashie or iron would have put them quite far
enough.

The same result often occurs through the
impatience which will not allow a woman to
call back her caddie when he has given her the
wrong club, and she plays the shot in consequence, hoping that the Goddess of Fortune
will aid her to bring off the stroke with the
desired result, even though the means are far
from what they should be.

Many a woman has lost a match, and particularly a medal-play competition, by playing

shot after shot with lightning rapidity. In a
bunker I have frequently seen ten or twelve
strokes used when, if a moment's study of the
situation had been taken, one or two would
have sufficed.

From the tee the average woman, who
plays an even moderately good game, usually
does consistently well, but if she does fail it is
from topping nine times out of ten. With
men, failure usually comes from slicing or
pulling, but I think that the average woman
drives a straight ball nearly always.

Topping is, of course, caused by taking the
eye off the ball a fraction of a second before
it is struck, and this is a fault which besets
women throughout every stroke from tee to
hole.

Women, at any rate all golfing women,
are pronounced optimists, and in their eager-
ness to see the ball go into the hole, they are
prone to lift their eyes for just that infinitesimal length of time that is too soon, and the
result is failure.

When one finds that the practice has become a settled habit, the only thing to do is to steel the mind rigidly against looking for the ball until at least a full second after it has been struck.

Many women accustom themselves to playing around without caddies, and this practice is responsible for much of the habit of looking up quickly to watch the flight of the ball.

Another very common fault among women is overgolfing.   The woman begins with a tremendous amount of enthusiasm, and she spends all her waking hours of daylight on the links for the first week or two.   She probably improves very rapidly in the first few days; then, as she grows stiff and sore from the unaccustomed exercise, she becomes disgusted with the game, temporarily at least, and it is perhaps a month or six weeks before its fascinations induce her to begin the weary road to success once more.

This is a practice much more common than

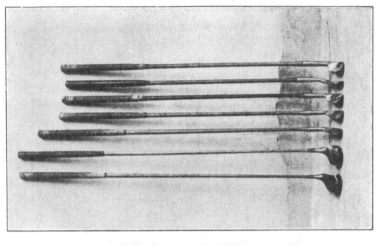

SIDE VIEW.

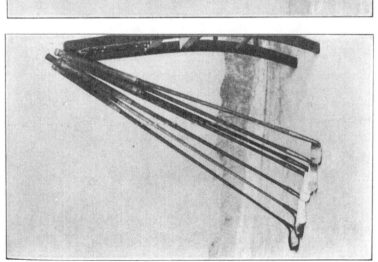

FRONT VIEW.

A SET OF MODERN CLUBS.

one would imagine, and whenever one hears of a woman who has tried golf, and is not enthusiastic over it, one may put her down as being in one of these intermediate stages.

The last of the faults which I think are common enough to be spoken of under this general caption is that of becoming nervous in the face of difficulties. It is astonishing to note how a woman who ordinarily will get away a drive of 150 yards with no trouble at all, will hesitate at an obstacle which requires a carry of perhaps but fifty yards. " He who hesitates is lost," is an axiom which everyone knows, and it is particularly true of golf.

The average woman falters in her mind as she sees the hazard loom up before her, and when she does that, in nine cases out of ten, she fails to carry it.

Yet it is not lack of pluck which causes this distressing effect. The average woman is, I think, far more plucky in the face of practically certain defeat than is the average man.

When did you ever see a man hammering away in dead earnestness when he was playing five more in a bunker and his opponent was ten yards off the green? Yet it is no uncommon sight in a woman's match.

CHAPTER II

THE first thing to do, if one wishes to play golf, is to read some good book on the game, in order to acquire a general understanding of what one is trying to do.

But no matter how good the book, one cannot become a crack golfer by sitting in the house and reading it. Theory is all very well, but it is practice that makes perfect in golf, as well as in everything else.

Practically every golf club in this country has in its employ a professional golfer, whose duties are to give instruction and repair clubs primarily, but who sometimes, at the smaller links, acts as green-keeper at well.

Usually he has played golf from the time he left off his swaddling-clothes, and he plays

41

it far more by instinct than by rhyme or reason. He plays a successful shot, not because
he wants to, but because he can't help it, as
an apoplectic old gentleman once remarked
indignantly, quite as though the " pro.'s "
skill was a personal affront to him.

There are only a half-dozen or so professionals in America who were not born and
bred at this game, and as a rule they have no
knowledge of any other, and some of them
are men of little education. They therefore
are unable to explain the faults which arise
from the natural efforts of the player to
master what she fondly believes is a St.
Andrews swing, and those which arise
from former flirtations with tennis or basket-
ball.

Ordinarily, it will be found, and curiously
so, that the best player is by no means the best
teacher, and two of the best instructors I know
cannot play eighteen holes within five strokes
of the average amateur of their clubs, but
they have acquired the knack of telling others

how to play, and of detecting the faults of their pupils. This last is really a much more valuable trait than the former, for, while a person may learn to do a thing from observation and imitation, she can't as easily correct a glaring fault in her play by watching an expert at work.

If you can get hold of an instructor who really has some idea of telling one how to play, it is best, I think, to begin at least under his instruction, but if you find that the " pro." has little or no idea of telling you how to achieve the desired result, or what you are doing wrong, it is better to leave him alone and work out your own salvation.

When you have decided that golf is an absolutely necessary adjunct to your peace of mind and happiness in this world, the first proceeding, after obtaining the proper clothes (is there any occupation whatever from birth to grave for which woman does not consider clothes the most necessary adjunct?), is to secure some of the implements of war.

For the proper playing of the game of golf there are six clubs necessary, viz., driver, brassey, cleek, mid-iron, mashie, and putter, and I have also known many golfers to whom a niblick was also useful at times. Besides these, many players carry a jigger and driving-mashie.

I shall content myself at present by giving the names of the necessary clubs, leaving them to be discussed at length under a separate chapter, and proceeding to generalize on the first day's proceedings.

While six clubs are necessary to the expert player, it is a great mistake for a novice to purchase so many to begin with. She should buy a driver and a lot of old balls. Don't take new ones, or you will wound your feelings deeply when your first shot cuts a gash an inch long and a quarter of an inch deep in the pretty white little globe.

Take the driver and the balls and proceed to a quiet spot, either with the " pro.," or, if you have decided to play out your own ideas, with no one but your conscience, and a caddie to chase the balls.

All the play that one indulges in for the first few days should be driving away the balls with the driver, and if one can command the self-control, it is wise to practice some time in merely swinging the club over a leaf or bit of paper on the ground instead of the ball. However, this is a precept which it is quite too much to expect the ordinary mortal to be able to follow.

The tortures of Tantalus are as nothing compared to those of the mortal who has once tasted the joys of a full cleanly hit shot, and if our tyro can be kept from setting out for a round of the links with the determination shining from her eye of lowering the medal record on her first appearance, she is doing quite all that one could expect.

This last practice is responsible for the wrecking of more promising golfing careers than anything else that one can do or leave undone, and I cannot emphasize too strongly its harmfulness.

Not only should the novice refrain from playing the course for several weeks, but, above all, she should never think of counting the number of her strokes for six months after she begins to play.

The temptation to do so is of course very great, but if she refrains from it the ultimate reward is quite compensation enough.

It is very hard to make a beginner understand why she should not keep track of her strokes, and thus note her improvement from day to day. The reason is that in an effort to save a stroke here or there, in order that one may cut one's record for nine holes from 125 to 124, the excited record-breaker will be led into committing numberless sins of commission and omission which she never would have dreamed of even, but for the fatal lodestar of a broken record luring her on.

One of these tricks may temporarily bring about the desired effect, but it is sure to be

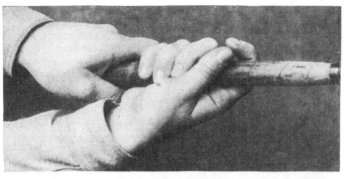

FIG. I.—THE FIRST STAGE.

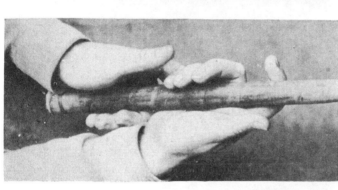

FIG. II.—THE SECOND STAGE.

THE DRIVING GRIP.

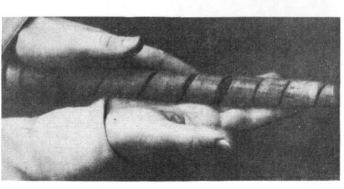

FIG. III.—THE THIRD STAGE.

only temporarily, and by the time she has a répertoire of several such, Miss Novice will find that she has forfeited all chance of ever making a respectable score except by an effort of the imagination which would make Baron Munchausen turn in his grave with envy.

After becoming comparatively accomplished with the driver, the novice may take up the cleek. The stroke for this club is made so much like a driver-shot that after one has mastered the rudiments of that club, the other will be very easy. After acquiring a bowing acquaintance with these two clubs, the mashie may be taken up. Go thirty or forty yards from a putting-green with a lot of old balls, and drop them at intervals on the ground, and proceed to play them up as near as possible to the hole. After they are on the green, you can add variety to the practice by getting out your putter and putting them into the hole.

Putting is a matter entirely of individual fancy. All the other strokes of golf are made on more or less general principles, but everyone is a law unto herself when once the putting-green has been reached.

With this knowledge of what to do in mind when the clubs are selected, let us proceed to consider the implements themselves.

CLUBS

In looking back to the days when I first began to golf, I remember that it was a matter of absolutely no importance to me whether my club was made of hickory or persimmon or cast-iron, and that I was far too impatient to get out on the links to stop to consider whether the advantages of a dogwood head outweighed those of one made of persimmon or vice versa. I assume that the majority of other girls feel as I did about it.

With this in mind I shall therefore eliminate, at this stage of writing at least, all discussion of a technical nature, and simply try to give a little useful advice in the matter

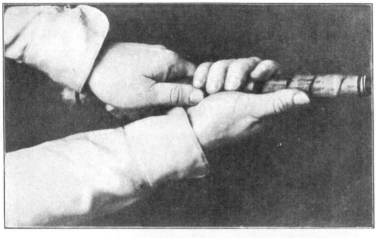

FIG IV.—THUMBS TOO FAR AROUND.

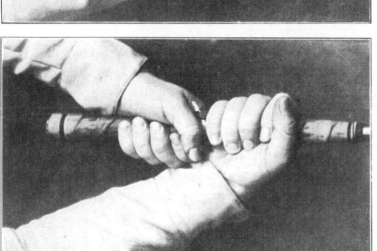

FIG V.—THUMBS STRAIGHT DOWN.

TWO FORMS OF BAD GRIP.

of selecting one's golfing tools from the ordinary dealer's or professional's stock.

The first, and by all odds the most important, point to be considered in selecting a driver (and the other clubs as well) is the balance. This is a matter which everyone must decide for herself, for one's strength of wrist plays a very large part in determining the proportionate weights in head and shaft which combine to make a club of ideal balance. It is a very difficult thing to obtain a club which " feels " exactly right, and sometimes a golfer will handle and " waggle " a hundred before finding one which seems as if it would do. Even then a trial on the links frequently shows that what seemed ideal in the professional's shop is far from it in actual play, and the whole work of selection must be gone through with once more.

It undoubtedly may seem absurd to the non-golfer, this care and attention to the fraction of an ounce in weight or of an inch in the length or slant of a club, but no golfer con-

siders it anything but a solemn duty and a
pleasure as well.

In fact, the club-makers' shops are always
full of players who stop in to handle and try
clubs, even when they have no intention of
purchasing them, but merely for the pleasure
of feeling a good club in their grasp.

For a player of average height—that is,
about five feet five inches for a woman, or
five feet nine inches in a man—a driver should
be from 37 to 41 inches in the first instance,
and from 40 to 44 inches in the second,
measuring of course from the extreme end of
the shaft to the sole of the club.

The " lie " (meaning the relation which the
sole of the club bears to the angle of the
shaft) which will give the player the greatest
power, combined, of course, with a fair degree
of accuracy, must be learned by each individual in actual practice. To begin with, it
is best to select a club which, when the entire
sole rests easily on the floor of the shop, brings
the shaft in the natural grip to a point where

it seems natural, and as though a full, powerful blow could be struck.

It is best not to go to extremes in selecting clubs. It may appear to one person a conclusion so logical that it admits of no denial that a limber or "whippy" shaft and a heavy head make a combination which will produce the best results, or it may appear with equal force to another that a light head and a stiff shaft are the ideal combination. Indeed, a dozen other variations may seem the one and only solution to the art of golf, but one of the uses of the game is to prove that there is no such thing as a logical deduction, and so it is best to start with clubs which are neither at the one extreme nor the other.

As a general thing, no beginner appreciates for a long time the strength required to swing a golf-club rapidly and swiftly, and she therefore selects clubs which seem perhaps very light when not in actual use, but are heavy when it comes to playing strokes.

Another point which at least ninety per

cent. of beginners fail to recognize is that it is the speed at which a club is traveling when it comes in contact with the ball, far more than its weight, which produces long drives. It is obvious that a lighter club can be swung faster than a heavy one, and as soon as the golfer has this point firmly imprinted on her memory, the sooner will she begin to drive nearer the 200-yard mark.

Still, the matter of light clubs should not be carried to extremes, any more than anything else. If there is no weight behind the swing the additional speed will be wasted just as certainly as weight is useless without speed.

The weight of the club once decided upon, the limberness of the shaft is the next consideration.

As a general rule, a whippy shaft will drive a trifle longer ball than a stiff one, but as the whippiness increases, so also does the tendency to slice and pull, and it is therefore best for the novice to begin with a club with a fairly stiff shaft.

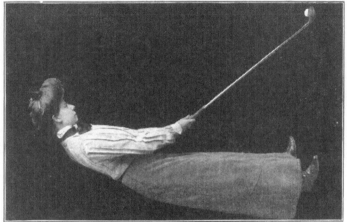

THE ADDRESS. SIDE VIEW.

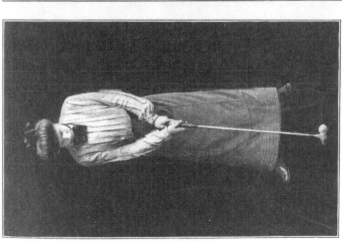

THE ADDRESS. FRONT VIEW.

The brassey is substantially the same as the driver, except that it is a trifle heavier, the face is a little more laid back, and it has its sole covered with a brass plate, perhaps a sixteenth of an inch thick. The shaft should also be a trifle stiffer than that of the driver, and about one inch shorter. Otherwise the clubs are the same, and the same reasons govern their selection.

Until reasonably expert the driver should be used only from the tee, and the brassey's usefulness begins as soon as it is necessary to obtain a long distance after the tee shot.

Even though the ball be lying badly, and it seems almost impossible to get it out, do not hesitate to use this club, for the brass on the sole will cut through the turf readily, and the loft of the face will throw the ball up sufficiently to get away a clean shot.

In selecting one's wooden clubs, it is well to remember that practical experiments have proven the fallacy of the idea that a driver or brassey which has a thick face possesses an advantage over a thin-faced one.

Indeed the latter is preferable from the fact that, with it, it is much easier to pick a ball out of a bad lie.

A moment's reflection shows the truth of this, for it is apparent that the nearer to the ground the center of the face is, so much the less does the ball need to be elevated for it to come in contact with the very center of the club.

The cleek is the next most powerful club on the list, and should be used to play distances between a full brassey and a mid-iron shot, or, say, when distances between 100 and 125 yards are to be covered.

It should also be used when the distance to be covered is greater, but the lie so bad that using a brassey seems but to invite disaster.

The shaft should be about as stiff as that of the driver, and the head laid back only a small fraction of an inch. Like the brassey and driver, and for the same reasons, the blade or face should be narrow rather than thick. The face should not be more than 3½ inches long, for if it is, it will detract from the club's ability to pick a ball out of a hole, without adding anything to its driving power.

The patent cleeks, in which the shaft runs through the socket to the sole, and in which the socket is but about an inch long, are rather more powerful driving clubs than those of ordinary pattern.

The mid-iron, to take the club with the next longest driving capacity, is, as its name implies, a club for moderate distances of from perhaps 80 to 100 yards.

The face should be lofted to an angle of about 45 degrees, rather broader in the face than the cleek. The extra loft throws the ball more into the air than do the aforementioned clubs, and therefore it has less run.

The mashie or approaching club has a face that is not only the deepest by one-half an inch of all the clubs, but it is laid back to an angle of 60 degrees. It should have a head heavier proportionately than any of the other clubs, and, like the rest, should have a stiff shaft.

All these clubs, as the illustrations show, are shorter in a descending scale, each one perhaps an inch less than the one mentioned before it.

What is sometimes called the most important club in the game is the putter, and here there are at least a dozen styles to choose from. Personally, I have found the best results from a heavy-headed gooseneck which has a very little slant to the face. The shaft should be comparatively short and absolutely stiff.

The niblick is the club of last resort, and when its use is necessary, the player is generally so desperate that " all niblicks look alike to her," to paraphrase a popular song of the day.

With the outfit of clubs selected, the next thing to do is to learn how to grip them correctly.

THE DRIVING GRIP

Take the driver and hold it so that the
sole lies flat on the ground at every point, and
the end of the handle rests against the skirt
half-way between the waist and knee.

Then place the hands on either side of the
handle, as shown in the illustration of the
driving grip, Fig. I. Care should be taken
to see that the shaft runs across the base of
the knuckles, and not the palm of the hand,
but under no circumstances, on the other hand,
allow the club to fall nearer the fingers than
the knuckles.

Fig. II. shows the method in which the
hands should close, and Fig. III. the com-
pleted grip.

This grip, I think, is by all odds the best.
Fig. IV. shows another which is used to some
extent, but it is impossible to get so good a
follow-through with it, and it also tends to
tighten the muscles of the arms in swinging
back for the stroke. This tightening extends

to the wrists, and prevents obtaining that subtle snap so essential to long driving.

Fig. V. shows the club correctly grasped with the fingers, but with the thumbs held down the shaft. This is a style which invariably takes from ten to fifteen yards from the length of the shot, although adding in some instances to its accuracy. So, on the whole, it is not to be recommended.

The relation of the hands to each other is a very important point, and the closer they are held, the longer the shot, for every inch they are apart lessens the drive by twenty yards at least.

Under any and all conditions the position of the left hand should remain the same, as illustrated in Figs. I., II., III., and IV.

The shaft should be grasped with the left hand as firmly as possible, and also with the last three fingers of the right hand. The forefinger and thumb should barely touch the club, and if at all only at the last second of the downward swing before the ball is struck.

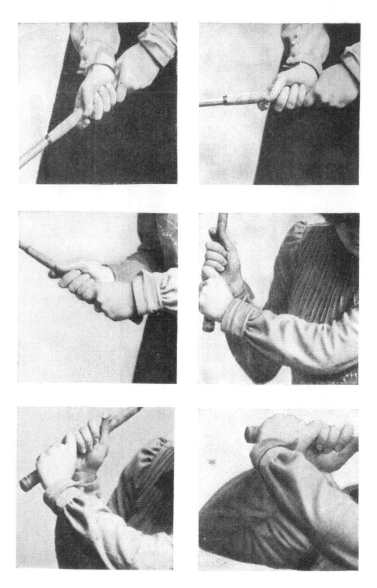

THE WRIST ACTION IN DRIVING.
The Up Swing

CHAPTER III

AFTER settling the question of the proper method of gripping the club to one's entire satisfaction, the next step in order is the determining of the relation the position of the feet shall bear to the ball, and the direction it is wished that the ball shall take.

This is technically called the stance, and there are almost as many ways of standing as there are of gripping the club.

The stance may be divided into three classes, which are called:

I.—Off the right foot.

II.—Off the left foot.

III.—Standing square.

The most common method is the first, and

probably so because the player can see the direction in which she wishes the ball to go better, and consequently feels more confidence that it will go there.

In adopting this stance, the right foot is placed in advance of the left, the exact difference depending upon the player's fancy. In other words, if a line were drawn on the ground parallel to the line of flight, the left toe should be just touching it, while the right would be anywhere from one to ten inches over it. The extent to which the right foot is advanced determines the proportion of the weight of the body it should hold; the farther it is advanced, the greater amount of weight is rested upon it.

In driving " off the left foot," the right foot is withdrawn in almost the same proportion as it is advanced when driving " off the right foot," and the stance is virtually the inverse of the former.

In standing square, the stance is as its name implies. Both feet are on a parallel line, and

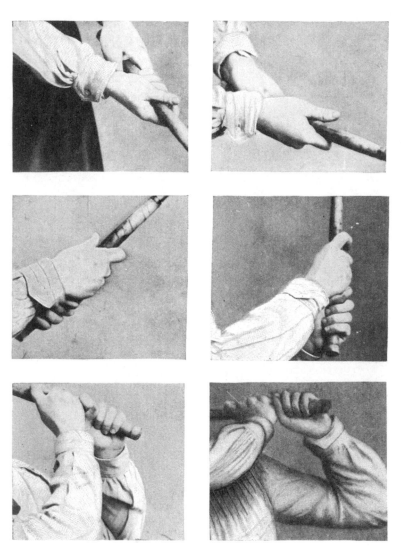

THE WRIST ACTION IN DRIVING.

The Finish.

the weight of the body is equally divided between them.

The distance which the feet should be apart
is another matter which must be decided by
the individual, and should be regulated by
both feeling and physique.

Roughly speaking, the feet should be from
18 to 24 inches apart.

The knees should be bent in the smallest
degree, just so that the knee-joint is not stiff,
and the arms, when the club head rests behind
the ball, are bent in an equally small degree
at the elbow.

The position of the ball and its relation to
the feet are most important.

When the " standing square " stance is
adopted, the ball should be nearly oppo
site the left heel—that is, within two or
three inches of the line which a right
angle drawn by the feet and ball would
make.

When playing " off the right foot " the
ball should be more to the right, and as the

foot is advanced, so proportionately should the ball be moved to the right.

When playing " off the left foot " the ball should be inversely moved to the left.

I favor using a stance in which the feet are practically on a line, as the illustration of the side view of the address for a drive will show. I do not, as I said before, try to place my feet in identically the same position for each shot, and therefore the position of the right one may occasionally vary an inch or even two inches, both in its distance to the right of the left foot and its distance ahead of the left.

Again, I try to have my feet approximately twenty inches apart, but I let the matter settle itself instinctively, and only try to get a stance which seems natural. The majority of the men who have written books on golf, and also the professionals, agree that it is only the position of the left foot which is really important, and that the right may vary in its place several inches without affecting the result of the shot; my experience has been that this is true.

Another point, perhaps a minor considera-tion, but one which many a beginner on the rocky pathway to golfing fame stumbles over, is the position of the toes. Some think that they must be turned out as nicely as a dancing professor insists upon in the first position; others think that the feet should be straight, and some imagine, or at least a casual ob-server would so suppose, that a good drive can only be secured by turning the toes in.

No one need worry over this point, how-ever, for as good drives may be made in one way as in another. Ordinarily I place the ball and I tee about three inches to the right of my left heel, and I rest the weight of my body equally on each foot. I have found that by adopting this stance I can obtain a full, easy backward swing, and that I can swing my club in a sweeping circle much farther and straighter in the line of flight of the ball— or, in technical words, can obtain a much

better " follow-through " in this way than in
any other.

The question of the " follow-through "
may seem of very little importance to the tyro,
but later on I shall endeavor to dissipate this
idea.   At the present time I shall content
myself with saying that it is an admitted fact
that it is quite as important as is the part of
the swing before the ball is struck.

The main objection to an accentuation of
the left-foot style is that it makes a proper
follow-through very difficult to achieve.
Owing to the right foot being so far back, it
is impossible to be facing front at the end of
the swing, and the body pivots on the left
foot, thereby encouraging the club to swing
round the body.   On the other hand, however, if the right foot is advanced too far,
the prospect of hooking the ball is almost
certain.   For these reasons, therefore, I
recommend that the right foot be only about
an inch ahead of the left, if at all; but every
player of any experience will soon pick out

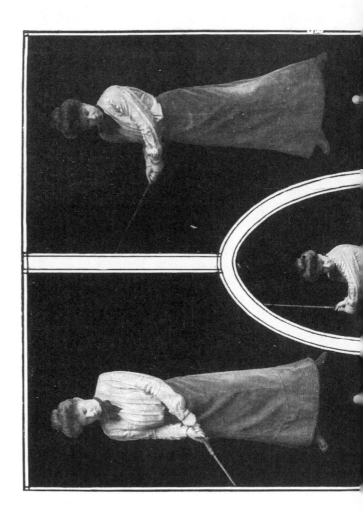

THE UP-SWING.

the position which for some reason, real or
fancied, seems to be a trifle the best, and use
it for the regular stance. When the time
comes, as come it will inevitably to even the
very best golfer in the world, that no shot
can be made as it should from that stance,
then simply try a little change in it, and you
will very soon find that you are once more
playing up to your game. When that day
comes that the new stance becomes another of
the failures and disappointments, try another,
and so you will gradually work around to the
old favorite once more. In other words, golf
is a continual experiment, and those who know
when to continue experimenting, and when to
be satisfied with the results already achieved,
make the best players.

Never made the mistake of taking up a
certain stance simply because some celebrated
golfer uses it. Be a law unto yourself, for,
unless you stand so that you feel natural and
easy and as though you were going to hit the
ball exactly as you wish, you never will be able

to do so. Confidence in golf is at least half
the battle. If you find that some champion
uses the same stance that you do, well and
good. Say to yourself, he uses good judgment and is a legitimate champion, and feel
well satisfied that the champion follows you,
but never follow him. When I say that, after
finding the stance which seems best, one
should continue using it, I do not mean that
one should worry over getting in exactly the
same position each time. I take up a stance
which is substantially the same, but I do it
instinctively, and never think of looking to
see just how many inches one foot is away
from the other, or how many inches one is
in front of the other.

There is no surer way of producing foozles
or of acquiring a stiff and awkward, to say
nothing of an improper, swing than to continually worry over getting in identically the
same position for every stroke.

The ball should be teed at whatever place
the club head lies when it is gripped in the

proper way, and then allowed to fall naturally to the ground straight in front of the player. The whole idea is to get it at such a distance that it will be directly in the line of a *natural* swing. There is a great diversity of opinion about the distance one should stand away. Some of the best drives in the country stand so far that the toe of their club, when addressing the ball, is quite two or three inches behind the ball, while others have the ball even with the neck of the club head. I do not favor either of these extremes.

If the ball is too far away and the player has to *reach* for it, as it were, the whole position is quite apt to be cramped, and the swing is consequently without snap, or else, in endeavoring to have it free and easy, the player does not always " reach " the exact fraction of an inch which is necessary for the perfect performance of the shot, and a bad slice or pull results.

With the question of grip and stance properly settled, in mind if not in actual prac-

tice, the next thing to consider is the swing
of the club, from which the force which drives
the ball is obtained.

As I have said before, the swing for all the
strokes of the long game, or, in other words,
those which are made with the full power of
the club in hand, depends upon fixed and in-
variable principles, however far good golfers
may differ from one another in matter of
detail in execution. The swing proper may
be divided into three component parts:

I.—The wrist action.

II.—The arm movement.

III.—The body movement.

Each plays its own particular part in the
achievement of the desired result, and no one
can hope to become a good long-game player
who has not mastered the intricacies of all
three.

While it is true that a mastery of all three
of the component parts of the swing is necessary to achieve long play, one of these parts
is a little more essential than the other two,

and vastly harder to master. This is the wrist action, and a perfect accomplishment of it is, I think, about the hardest bit of all the hard things in golf. But it is well worth working for, because when it is finally mastered, it will be found to have lengthened the wooden-club shots at least fifteen yards, and the full iron shots proportionately.

In the discouraging moments when it seems absolutely impossible to impart that almost undefinable snap to the wrists as the club head meets the ball, it may seem that a gain of fifteen yards is not worth anything like the trouble it is causing, but when you come to play in a tournament or a match, on the wining of which your heart is set, that extra fifteen yards will seem worth anything in the world.

The illustrations which show the positions of the hands and wrists at the different stages of the upward swing give a far better idea of how the wrists should bend than words can do. As they show, the wrists should be supple from the very beginning of the stroke, and should be allowed to turn in a perfectly natural way. There are two benefits to be derived from this turning. The first lies in the fact that through it the club can be swung at a greatly accelerated speed, and, as I have pointed out in a former chapter, it is the speed of the swing which produces the distance of the shots; the second, that it is only through the turning of the wrists, as the club swings backward, that they can be brought into position for the impartation of a snap to the club as it meets the ball.

By glancing at the illustrations of the down swing it will be seen that at a couple of feet from the ball the wrists are bent. Just at this point they should be suddenly straightened and made rigid, and as this is done with the club moving at tremendous speed it has the effect of imparting a snap to the shot. Do not, however, fall into the error of supposing that because you have accomplished this much there is nothing more to worry

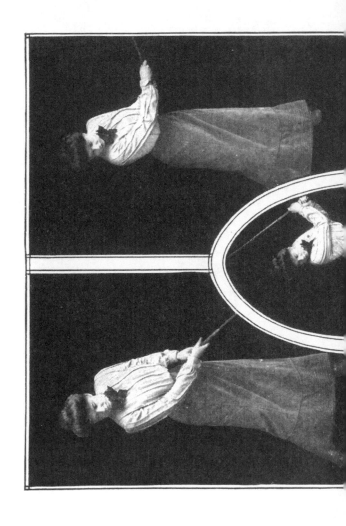

THE FOLLOW-THROUGH.

about, for nothing is further from the actual truth. The follow-through of a stroke, while not *quite* so important as the backward swing, plays a very essential part in the shot, much more so than anyone but a golfer of experience could believe.

After the ball is struck—and care should be taken to see that the desire to impart the " snap " to the shot does not impair the harmony of the swing (a point to be treated in the next chapter)—the hands and arms should swing well forward, and as the club moves onto the upward half of its circle the wrists will begin to perform another turn, exactly the reverse of that made in the backward stroke. That is, they will do so if they have been relaxed as soon as the ball has been struck. The illustrations show how the wrists should turn.

Many players are afraid to hold the wrists relaxed for fear that, if they do, the club's face will be diverted from the angle at which the ball was addressed, and that it will consequently connect with the ball in such a way as to cause a slice or pull.   This is a groundless fear.   If the club is gripped properly, the stance correct, and the wrists allowed to turn naturally, they will take care of themselves in the downward swing.   One should not, however, try to force this turn or disaster *will* result.   It won't be natural.

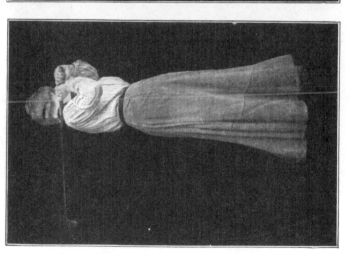

FINISH OF SWING (BACK VIEW).

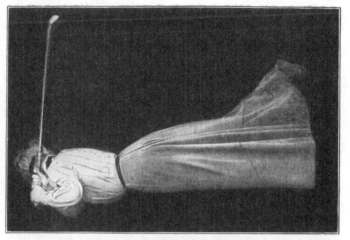

TOP OF SWING (BACK VIEW).

CHAPTER IV

THE SWING

IN the foregoing chapter I laid no stress upon the fact that the left wrist, in consequence of gripping the club more tightly with that hand than with the right, did a rather greater share of the work than the right, but this is nevertheless the case. The ideal, of course, is to have the two hands work so harmoniously together that it is impossible to see where one contributes more strength than the other.

With the theoretical knowledge of the part which the wrists should play in the full stroke firmly implanted in one's mind, the next step is naturally to apply the knowledge to a practical use, and like so many other things, it will be found that what works well in theory does not act quite so well in practice.

Of course the stronger the wrist muscles

are, the more power they will be able to exert, and with a realization of the important part which they play throughout the entire game from tee to hole in mind, it is the part of wisdom to spend a few moments each day in simple exercises which are calculated to develop them and the muscles, also, of the forearm. Any gymnasium or Delsarte teacher can suggest some good ones which can be practiced at home with dumbbells, or even without anything in the hands at all. Of course if one is in the habit of attending a gymnasium regularly, the wrist-machine will, as its name implies, give a great variety of wrist and forearm exercises.

One very beneficial exercise is to hold the arms out straight from the shoulders, and open and shut the fingers rapidly. In this the arm muscles should be held tense. Another good exercise is to hold the arms either extended or bent at the elbow, and relaxing completely the muscular tension at the wrists, shake the hands rapidly.

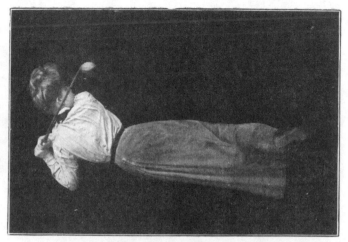

TOP OF SWING (SIDE VIEW).

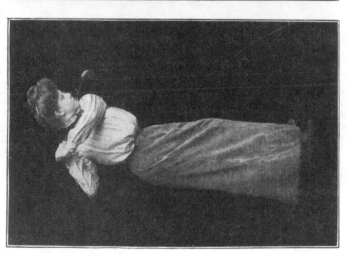

FINISH OF SWING (SIDE VIEW).

The second part of a correct full stroke depends upon the way the arms are swung. They must be free, and carry the club in as great an arc as possible, but in the endeavor to do this, accuracy and harmony must not be sacrificed. In fact, the harmony or perfect timing of the swing, and the exertion of strength at exactly the proper moment have much more to do with the success of the shot than has the amount of strength which is put into it.

As I said when writing about the stance, the distance the ball should be from the feet, when addressing it, is a matter for each individual to settle for herself, but it should be great enough to allow of the arms hanging clear and free from the body. In the first part of the backward stroke, as a glance at the accompanying illustration of the up-swing will show, the arms are already extending as far backward as they can without overbalancing the body or causing it to sway in the same direction. I shall later take up the part which the body plays, but for the moment I will touch only upon the arm movements.

After assuming the proper stance, it is a good idea to " waggle " the club two or three times over the ball, but it should never be " lifted " more than an inch over it. This is also a very good exercise for the wrists, and can be practiced as such to good advantage. After waving the club backward and forward two or three times to get the proper *feel* to it, rest for the space of a second behind the ball, and then begin the backward swing. To digress from this for a moment, let me solemnly urge everyone not to fall into the exceedingly bad habit of taking up several minutes in addressing the ball.

And there are any number of reasons why my advice on this point should be taken, even if it is scorned upon every other. In the first place, it is bad for the stroke one is to play, for it is tiring to eye, nerve, and muscle to make three or four feints, and consequently, when the actual stroke is played it is apt to be just a shade less effectual than if all this extra exertion had not been made. That this is the general opinion also among ninety-nine out of every hundred amateurs of the first class is, I think, a fact, and I also am unable to recall to mind a single professional of recognized ability who indulges in long-drawn-out preparations for his shot.

This is the argument against it from the purely practical standpoint of the question, but from the standpoint of courtesy and etiquette it is even more strong.

A player who wastes two or three minutes in addressing the ball for each shot will not only keep her partner standing in idle and of course helpless wrath, but she will probably keep back, and in a like degree of impotent rage, all the others who have been so unfortunate as to tee off behind her. According to the wording of the rules of golf, the player has as long as she likes to make her round, but if she wishes to be unpopular on the links she can take no quicker or more sure method

of achieving it than to indulge in this practice.

I may perhaps appear to feel too strongly
over this point, but anyone who has been
subjected to the annoyance of waiting and
waiting after each shot, while someone a
couple of hundred yards ahead goes through
a half-dozen meaningless swings, will, I
think, most heartily indorse all that I have
said.

After this bit of advice let us return to the
question of what part the arms are to play in
the achievement of a perfect swing. At the
beginning of the club's swing, for the first
three or four inches of its journey, the wrists
perform the work of raising it, as a glance
at the first illustration in the up-swing series
will show. At that point, as the next cut illustrates, the arms begin to assert themselves,
and they should be allowed to move *out*
freely. Under no circumstances, however,
allow the club head to swing *up*. On the contrary, when the club begins the backward

swing, keep it as close as possible to the ground. There are many important reasons for this. In the first place, this will carry the arms out *naturally* quite a little further than they would go if the club head went up more perpendicularly, and thus a larger arc of a circle is formed.

The advantages of this are at once obvious. The more distance that the club head travels on a line parallel with the ball, the less chance there is of it striking the ball above or below it (technically sclaffing or topping), and, of course, this is one point of danger eliminated.

Another advantage is that the further the club head travels on a line parallel to the ball, before striking it, the greater power it will impart to it. This, of course, is due to the fact that the momentum will be applied more directly behind the ball, and therefore utilized to its fullest extent. If, on the other hand, the club is coming down more perpendicularly, part of its momentum will be expended in covering that distance, and even when it hits the ball, it will do so with a sort of cut which will take many and many a yard from the length of the shot.

As the club head draws back, the arms follow, but the elbows should not be allowed to get too far away from the side of the body. Just how far (to the number of inches) they may be allowed to go, no one could specify, but a glance at the illustrations in the series showing the up-swing will give an idea. So much for the arms.

The third of the three component parts of the swing, the body movement, embraces not only the turning of the trunk of the body from the hips as the club swings up or down (when the body must sway, too), but also the degree in which the knee should bend and the heel turn.

After assuming the proper stance for addressing the ball, in which, as I stated in the chapter devoted to the stance, the knee should be bent just sufficiently to make the whole position easy, and to allow the body to turn

to the right as the club swings backward in
the upper part of the stroke, and to the left
as it completes the arc, swing the club backward, keeping in mind the idea that it must
be kept as close as possible to the ground.
As it swings, there will develop a strong
inclination to turn the entire body from the
knees up in the same direction. This should
never be done, however. With the hips as
a pivot, the trunk of the body may be allowed
to turn, but never more than is shown in the
illustration. In fact a little less would be
much preferable to the slightest degree more.

Perhaps the best guide as to the distance
the arms should be raised is that the club,
when at the very top of the swing, should
be a very little past the horizontal line back
of and across the right shoulder. As the body
turns, and the club swings up, the left heel,
if allowed to do so, will naturally raise itself
a few inches from the ground, and the foot
turn on the toe. This is all very well if not
carried to excess, but care must be taken to

see that only the natural turn is allowed, and that there is no forcing of it.

When the club has reached the extreme height to which the backward swing is to extend, without pausing for a single second, bring the arms and body around again in the same arc of the circle, and " sweep " the ball away. It is not a blow. It is distinctly a sweep, and this is a most important fact to bear in mind.

Many persons are imbued with the idea that after the ball is struck, it matters not what becomes of the club, or in what manner the arms and body finish out the stroke.

No greater mistake could be made. The follow-through of the stroke is considered nearly if not quite as important as that part of the stroke made before the club comes in contact with the ball, and a moment's reflection upon the laws of physics will demonstrate conclusively that this must be true.

If a ball and a club head are placed in contact with no force, it will be quickly seen that the point of contact is exceedingly small —no larger in fact than the point of a lead-pencil. On the other hand, a glance at the club head after a full stroke has been made often shows a mark of the ball which is at least as large as a quarter of a dollar.

The composition of which the ball is made has, of course, a certain amount of resiliency, and the wood of the club head also gives a fraction of an inch under the force of a full stroke. Consequently, when these two forces meet each other, it is proof that they are in actual contact for a certain period of time after the club head strikes the ball, and while this period is, of course, an infinitesimal part of a second, the club is traveling so fast that its relative position to the ball during that space is of the utmost importance.

Naturally, to achieve the perfect perform-ance of the shot, the head should be at an absolute right angle to the desired line of flight, and the further the club can be made to follow in this line, the better.

Consequently, after the ball is struck, the hands and arms should be allowed to swing as far forward as they naturally wish to go, as the illustrations in the series showing the follow-through, illustrate very clearly. And they also show that after the club has swung a couple of feet or a yard past the spot where the ball was, the wrists will begin to turn once more in the inverse way to that in which they turned as the club swung backward, and the finish of the stroke, if correctly carried out, will be the exact reverse of the top of the backward swing.

There are two great points, however, either of which, if neglected, will bring to naught the best efforts of the player, no matter how diligently she practices or how perfectly she acquires the swing.

They sound delightfully simple, but like many other things which seem simple, are tremendously intricate. They are:

First—Don't move your head.

Second—Keep your eye on the ball.

So important are these two injunctions that words fail to express their significance. Neglect of either, however, will teach it, and teach it in a way to demonstrate that the old saying that experience is a bitter teacher was a most true one.

The reason " why " these two things are of such importance I shall endeavor to satisfactorily explain in the next chapter.

In the meantime, burn into your mind with flaming letters:

" Keep your eye on the ball."

" Don't move your head."

The Caddy Has His Eye on the Ball

CHAPTER V

THE SWING *(continued)*

IT may seem that there are so many injunctions in golf to be kept in mind that
there cannot be any one point which it
is especially imperative to observe, but such
is, nevertheless, the fact, and it is the first
of the two injunctions I exhorted all golfers
to burn into their minds with flaming letters
at the conclusion of the preceding chapter:

" Keep your eye on the ball."

Six little words, but what a tremendous
amount they mean!

Oh, the sorrows which would have been
averted had the injunctions which they record
been strictly adhered to! The tears which
need not have been shed; the matches which
would not have been lost; the six-inch putts
which would not have been missed; the drives

which would not have been topped or pulled
or sliced or sclaffed!

The things which otherwise would not have
been are legion; far too numerous to count.
But perhaps it is better that we are but
human, and that the eye *will* wander. Were
it not so, golf would be so perfect a pleasure
and so great a delight that it might lose part
of its charm, for in it, as in everything else,
it is the unobtainable which is most desired.

It might seem to a hasty observer that if
one kept either the head immovable or the
eye on the ball, that the other essential would
follow as a matter of course, but such is by
no means the case. It is more apt to occur,
of course, but by no means is it a certainty.

Of the two, I consider keeping the eye on
the ball by far the most important, for if it
is done absolutely, the chances are very likely
that the head will be kept still.

There is no greater temptation in all the
world of golf than to take the eye off the
ball a fraction of a second before the club

comes in contact with it, in order that one may see where it is going as a result of the stroke. Women have from the days of Eve been accused of unlimited curiosity, but I am happy to say that I find from personal experience that men are much more apt to take their eyes off than women, and that, therefore, feminine curiosity, in golf at least, is second to man's.

I consider this point of such extreme importance that I earnestly advise all beginners to not only keep the eye on the ball until it is struck, but to keep it on the spot until the club has reached the end of the follow-through.

Nor need this advice be considered applicable to beginners only. Players of a considerable amount of skill may find that their game improves amazingly by following it, and while I myself confess that I do not, when in good form, follow it quite to the extent of not moving my eye until my club has reached the extreme end of the stroke,

I do so whenever I find that my game is not up to my best form.

The expression "keeping the eye on the ball," however, should not, in my opinion, be taken with too absolute literalness. I think that the eye should be focused not on the top of the ball, where it naturally would be if the ball were its object point, but on a spot of ground directly behind the ball itself. One advantage of this is that one is less apt to top the shot, and another that in this way the object upon which the eye has been focused is not swept away at the middle of the shot, as it is if the eye is directly upon the ball, and it is in consequence much easier to keep it steadier until the end of the follow-through has been reached. Although we are dealing just now with the importance of this point in its relations to the long game (as full shots with any distance-covering clubs are termed), it is equally important in every department of the game, down to six-inch putts, a point which I shall endeavor to impress when the other shots are being discussed. Of its corollary, keeping the head in the same position, its value lies in the fact that if this is done, the body will not sway as the club goes back on the up-swing, and hands, arms, and clubs must therefore swing down on the same positions as those which they had assumed in addressing the ball, and which it naturally follows assures the ball being struck in the absolutely correct way.

So thoroughly and entirely is this true that it is no uncommon feat for a professional, after assuming his stance and getting the correct address to the ball, to allow himself to be blindfolded, and then drive nearly as effective a shot as though his eyes were open. This, however, is something which can only be acquired by years of constant play, but it illustrates the importance of keeping the head still.

If the player were only satisfied to drive a moderately long ball, and paid much more attention to the correct carrying out of these details than to the amount of strength put into the stroke in an endeavor to make the records of James Braid, Douglas Rolland, and their like look insignificant, respectable driving from the tee through the green would not be such a difficult art, but ninety-nine out of every hundred players are not satisfied with this, and, in the endeavor to utilize every atom of strength, sway back an inch or two. There are several methods of practice which will overcome this fault.

A very excellent one, which has the advantage of being easy to take up at home, if you are so fortunate as to have a full-length mirror or a room large enough to allow of the swinging of a club in it without interference with bric-à-brac and furniture, is to practice swinging in front of the mirror, needless to say without a ball. Then by looking up at one's reflection instead of directly at the spot where the ball should be, the movement of the head can be detected.

This, of course, has the disadvantage of

taking the eye from the spot it should be in the actual stroke.

Another method, and probably a better one, is to assume a position on the tee with the sun directly at one's back, and watch the shadow of the head during the swing. In this way one can instantly tell whether it is being held immovable or not, and if not, the swing must of course be practiced until the desired result is achieved.

The matter of practicing is another point which should be considered seriously, and not done haphazard.

PRACTICING

There is only one way in which a person can become a really high-class golfer, and that is by constant and thoughtful practice. The idea that it is the person who plays the most rounds of a course who will be the best player is entirely erroneous. It makes little difference in the improvement to be sought, how many times a player makes a certain shot, if each time it is not made correctly, and in fact it is worse to play constantly in bad form than not to play at all.

The golfer who really wishes to improve will make it a point to practice over and over again for ten or fifteen minutes at a time the same shot, be it drive, approach, or putt, and study the cause and effect of each one.

It is unwise to practice one style of shot more than fifteen minutes in succession, however, for the muscles become a trifle tired from repeating the same motion time after time, and one also becomes a trifle careless, no matter how much this is guarded against.

To a person who reads this without stopping to think, it may seem that playing the regular round would be as good practice as the above method, but in the regular round you make a certain shot, and then have no opportunity of repeating it for five or ten minutes, in which time you have played a half-dozen or more other shots of an entirely different nature.

When one is trying to acquire the proper
swing for a stroke, it is by no means necessary
that a ball should be used.   In fact, it is often
a good idea not to do so, for so weak is human
nature, that the desire to make a fine drive out
of the shot becomes overpowering, and in consequence the result becomes of more importance than the method of achievement.

A good substitute for the ball is a leaf, a
bit of paper, or a cork, or anything, in fact,
which will serve as an object point for the
eye to focus upon.

An Easy Shot

CHAPTER VI

THE LONG GAME

THE four greatest obstacles to perfect driving are sclaffing, topping, pulling, and slicing, and any one of them is wonderfully easy—except when one really wishes to do so.

With the exception of taking the eye off the ball or swaying the head with the movement of the body in the swing, there is probably nothing in the glossary of golf which causes so much trouble as an improper stance.

As it may seem, both sclaffing and its very reverse, topping, may be caused by the same fault, viz., standing too much in front of the ball, that is, with it placed nearly opposite the right foot instead of nearly opposite the left. The results of this kind of a stance are at once apparent in one's play, and the result could easily be imagined if the player stopped to consider cause and effect.

The first result of such a stance is that the swing becomes a " chop " instead of a sweep, and the club comes down either upon the top of the ball or under it instead of being swept away just as the club head begins to rise.

The " pop-up " shot, which starts away from the tee with such promise, rises high in the heavens, and drops with such a disagreeable and annoying thud about fifty or one hundred yards short of where one expected from its fine start it was going to do, is caused by this kind of a choppy swing, as is also that most distressing of all things, a ball which runs with apparently tremendous speed along the ground, and loses itself in the first hazard upon the course.

Pulling and slicing, two faults from which only the really first-class player is free, may be caused by an improper stance, but usually are the result of not forcing the arms and shoulders to finish out the stroke in the line of flight taken by the ball.

This may happen from allowing the body to fall away from the ball as the club reaches it in the downward swing, or it may be due to pulling the arms around quickly to the left. If this is done, and the ball be struck squarely in the center of the club head, a terrific pull will result, while, if the arms have commenced to swerve enough to the left to cause the ball to be struck on the toe of the club, an equally great slice will result.

The difference in cause is so slight, and that of result so great, that it takes an experienced player to recognize that both are caused by practically the same error.

Other little faults which from time to time creep into a player's game, and for a longer or shorter time prevent the perfect execution of a drive, will be found to be due to a looseness of grip, or a carelessness regarding the way the thumbs are held, which may cause the club to turn in the hands.

Another common cause for a slice or pull is that the club is not evenly soled when addressing the ball, and in consequence it is at an angle when brought into contact with the ball in the swing.

This is a more important point than many players believe, and the beginner especially should invariably be sure that both the heel and toe are on the ground, and that the face is at right angles to the tee.

Another common fault is that of loosening every muscle of the body, and trying to get every particle of strength and weight into the stroke. This can only be done after a player has acquired a good share of proficiency, and while I by no means recommend that a player should endeavor to swing with no suppleness at all, I think it is better to err at first on the side of rigidity.

Despite all these precautions, however, there will come a time when a drive cannot be made as it should be, and then there is only one thing to do.

Adopt a half-swing, and try to make up for the lack of distance the club travels before reaching the ball by accuracy and power of the follow-through.

With half a swing this is absolutely necessary in order to get any distance at all, and the practice will be found very beneficial to the length of the drive when a full swing is resumed, as well as being absolutely the only method of playing when the unhappy time of being unable to drive with a full swing arrives, as it undoubtedly will.

PLAYING AGAINST THE WIND

Nothing is more discouraging than to drive off what you consider a fine ball, and then have a wind take it away to one side, or else stop it at something like half the distance you felt sure it would go. The wind is a far more powerful factor than would seem possible, considering the size of the ball upon which it has to operate, and while its baleful influences cannot always be entirely overcome,

they can in most cases be rendered comparatively harmless, and in some few instances
made actually helpful.

When playing against a wind which is directly in one's teeth, the player should remember that the slightest pull or slice will be
magnified by the wind one-hundredfold, and
accuracy should therefore be the first consideration.

To obtain this one must of course maintain
a perfect balance on the feet, and the best way
to insure this is to swing easily—not try
to put an extra amount of force into the
stroke, as so many unthinking players do. If
the ball is hit absolutely clean, and the follow-
through is all that it should be, the drive will
be within a few yards as far as though you
had hit it with all your strength, and it is certain that while a " pressed " shot may once in
a dozen times be phenomenal, the eleven failures will be more than ordinarily bad.

It is true that a low ball hit in the right
way will travel much further against a wind

than a high ball, but it will not do so if its lowness is the result of a half-top. Trying to *half* top a ball causes more fully topped shots than one could count, and even if it is done successfully, the ball will not travel very far.

One should use a low tee under any and all circumstances, and if this is done, a correctly hit ball will not fly high enough for the wind to have much of an effect upon it.

With the wind directly at one's back the same rules remain in force, except that perhaps the tee might be made a fraction of an inch higher, in order that the ball may get up in the air a little more, and so give the wind an opportunity to exert its force.

When the wind is blowing across the line of play, it may be made an aid by noticing whether it is blowing from left to right, or right to left, and playing for a slice or a pull as the case may be. By so doing one obtains in many instances nearly as much benefit from the wind as though it had been from behind. It is so easy, and at times apparently so unavoidable, to slice and pull that it may seem like carrying coals to Newcastle to give advice on how to commit these chief sins of the golfing decalougue, but there are times when they have their uses the same as everything else.

To pull a ball, the best method is to place the ball very little farther back than usual, aim very slightly to the right, and hit clean, exactly as though you wished to drive a straight ball. If properly carried out, this method will give quite enough pull to the shot to insure its keeping a little bit more than straight against the wind, and it will have, when it strikes the ground, the rotary motion toward the left which is responsible for the long roll which all pulled balls have. In fact, so much farther does a pulled drive go than even an absolutely straight one, that the majority of the best players endeavor to impart a slight pull to every long shot they may be called upon to make, except, of course, where the character of the links makes a pulled shot liable to run into a hazard.

A common method pursued when it is wished to pull a shot is to stand well in front of the ball and aim well to the right. This is a very bad policy, for it will result in so terrific a pull that it is impossible to gauge the distance it will cover, and much trouble is likely to follow its use.

Another argument against its adoption is that, if one takes up this stance, the mind will instinctively think about achieving a pull, and the shoulders in consequence will instinctively swing around to the left, in order to help in the desired result, instead of leaving it to be accomplished by the stance, and the resultant pull will be quite too strong to be pleasant or useful.

Slicing a ball when the wind is blowing from left to right (of course I refer invariably to right-handed players) is one of the most difficult and delicate strokes of the games. The reason that it is more so than is a pull comes from the fact that it is easier to overdo it, and also that the wind has much more effect upon it.

When playing for a slice, aim a little to the left, and keep the ball well in front of you, almost opposite the left foot, and then play your shot exactly as though a straight drive were desired. If such a thing is possible, the follow-through is even more important than anywhere else.

It may be thought that I have devoted too much space and gone into too many details in analyzing the movements which are combined in the perfect performance of the drive, but if one stops to consider that the stroke is really the fundamental principle upon which are based all the other full strokes of the game, it will be realized that it would be impossible to dwell too strongly upon so important and far-reaching a point.

It is far too much to expect that the golfer will be possessed of sufficient self-restraint to refrain from making the rounds of the course after having once acquired a fairly proficient command of the driver, and I shall therefore proceed to offer some hints of a general character before taking up the technical points in which lie the secrets of the brassey and cleek

AMOUNT TO PLAY

The amount that a person can play and yet keep at the top of her game depends absolutely on the individual physique and mental temperament. Generally speaking, if one devotes a half hour to practicing certain shots over and over again, and follows this practice with an eighteen-hole round of the links three times a week, it is quite enough to obtain the best results. Still, the point, like so many others, must be determined by the player personally.

I think it rather better to play eighteen holes three times a week than thirty-six holes on two days, unless one is fortunate enough to be able to reach the club with a very short journey, for most golfers will find it necessary to spend from an hour to an hour and a half traveling before reaching the links, and this trip added to thirty-six holes of golf over the long course and the return trip to town makes a little more exertion than is beneficial to the average woman. Still, if the course is easy to walk over, and a trial finds you fresh and energetic after such a day's golf, there is no reason why your play should not be done in this way.

OVERGOLF

There is one point over which the golfer who really desires to improve will come to grief more surely than she who is not so enthusiastic, and the more earnest the player, the more certainly is she in danger of shipwreck in this Scylla of golf. This is the matter of playing too much. Once you feel you are overgolfed, lay aside your clubs, no matter what the temptation to play, for several days, or a week is better if your moral strength is of sufficient caliber to withstand such a strain, and banish the thought of golf from your mind. It may be the hardest bit of self-denial you have ever accomplished, but it will pay in the long run.

There is absolutely nothing which will bring disaster on the links and despair to your heart so quickly and fiercely and everlastingly as trying to play when overgolfed.

The novice may think I speak too strongly, but I assure her I do not. Nothing goes right. Your drives are sliced or pulled or topped or sclaffed, your approaches the same. Your putts simply will not go into the hole. Or if they do go in, they will not stay there. They roll around the edge of the cup and hang on the lip, and seem to grin at you with fiendish delight, and the more care you take, the worse matters become. There is but one remedy. Stop playing, and the sooner you realize it the better it will be both for your game and your conscience.

ACCURACY

Next to a good style, the most important
thing to aim for is accuracy of direction. It
makes little difference whether one is five
yards more or less distant from the tee after
a drive, provided the ball has gone straight
for the hole and is lying on the fair green in
the center of the course, but if it is in the long
grass, or other trouble which almost invariably is to be found on either side of the
line of play, the added five yards of distance
which lands one here will be found very
costly, for it will take a stroke to get out of
the trouble, and another to reach the point
where a good second after a straight drive
would have placed the ball.

The same principle is exemplified when the
green is within reach. A straight shot reaches
it, and then the orthodox two putts should see
one down, while a wildly played approach will
necessitate a little approach putt and usually
the other two as well, the distinct loss of a
stroke.

One of the best methods to insure accuracy is to never " press," but use a club which will give the desired distance with an easy swing.

Thus, if pressing with a cleek will achieve the desired result, take a brassey; if a mid-iron might do it, take a cleek; and so on down the list of clubs.

CHAPTER VII

THE LONG GAME (*continued*)

UPON every golf-course there should be, and almost invariably is, a proportion of holes so long that it will require two, or even three, shots with the full power of the driver to reach the green.

The point of arranging the distance of the holes on a golf-course so that it is necessary to play shots perfectly in order to reach the green in two or three or four, as the case may be, is a most important one for the development of good golf, but one which is, most unfortunately, only too often overlooked. It is so manifestly unfair to have a hole of such a distance that a player can make a poor drive and still reach the green in two by making a good brassey, and be just as well off as a player who has made a good drive and a good approach shot with a mashie, that it is very discouraging to the good player, and to play over a course so arranged takes away much of the pleasure of the game.

Supposing, however, that the course has been correctly laid out and the distance arranged so that full shots with the driver are required, the point arises, as soon as a bad lie is found, of what club to use which will not only lift the ball out of the bad lie, but has the power to achieve the desired distance. The club designed for the express purpose is the brassey. Of course, where the lie is good enough, the driver should be used, but when there is any doubt whatsoever of the ability to get the ball away with the driver the brassey should be taken.

This club is really like a driver, except that its face is usually laid back a trifle so as to impart a loft to the ball, and on its sole is fastened a thin piece of brass.

In playing a brassey, practically the same swing should be used in the drive proper, except that it should not be allowed to swing back quite so far.

In driving a ball from a tee, one should endeavor to hit it as cleanly as possible, but when the lie is such that a brassey is being used, one should not endeavor to do this.

On the contrary, the club should be brought down more perpendicularly, and the ground struck at the same time with the ball.

In playing a brassey, do not imagine that because the ground should be struck as well as the ball, an extra amount of force must be imparted to the stroke.

Rather to the contrary, for the whole secret of successfully negotiating a bad lie is the cleanness with which the ball is picked up, and, as I have reiterated in former chapters, the " follow-through."

In addressing the ball for a brassey-shot, it should be a trifle nearer the right foot than when a tee shot is being played, and that foot should also be somewhat further advanced than in the other instance. It may sound absurd to say that one inch is about the distance, but a golfer will readily appreciate the difference which such an even apparently insignificant distance will make.

If the player has been wise enough to accustom herself to the use of a low tee she should have no difficulty in hitting her brassey-shots cleanly, but if she has been accustomed to driving off from a mound of sand anywhere from one to three inches in height, she will probably find that the brassey-shots are being topped most distressfully. This is one of the punishments of using a high tee, and should offer an argument in favor of a low one, sufficiently strong to make the golfer discard that violation of the traditions of golf at once and for evermore, and the argument is equally applicable to all the shots played through the field.

The best way to remedy the fault, after discarding the high tee, is to fasten the eye on a spot directly behind instead of upon the ball when preparing for a stroke, as was ad-

vised in the first place. This has the effect of
bringing the objective focus of the eye to a
spot a trifle lower than in the other method,
and the result is that the club is instinctively
swung a little lower, bringing it down to the
proper level.

Sometimes a player will strike the ground
so hard a blow, in endeavoring to avoid topping, that the wrist will receive a severe jar,
and the memory of it will cause the player to
err on the other side, with the result that a
long series of " tops " will result.   There is
only one way to overcome this, and that is to
play the shots easily and carefully until the
feeling of flinching disappears.

If one is sclaffing brassey-shots continually
in an effort to avoid topping, it may be overcome by looking at a spot just ahead of the
ball, on the same principle that constant
topping may be overcome by looking behind it.

Beyond these points the advice laid down
for the performance of a drive, the timing of

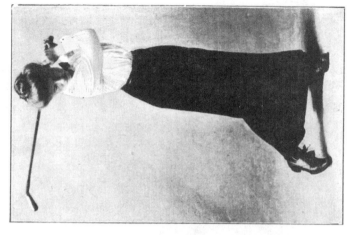

TOP OF CLEEK SHOT.

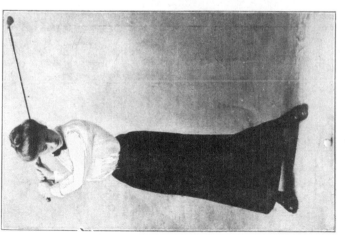

FINISH OF CLEEK SHOT.

the stroke, the necessity of accuracy, etc., etc., applies equally to the brassey.

One of the hardest " lies " from which to negotiate a good shot is from what is called a " hanging lie," that is, when the ground behind the ball slopes upward. The ball may be perched upon a tuft of grass which sets it up as high as though it were on the tee, but nevertheless it is an extremely difficult and unpleasant situation. The only way to negotiate it successfully is to allow the club to go through after the ball in accordance with the dip of the ground; and another thing to be very particular about here, and in the performance of every other stroke as well, is to see that the face of the club is not turned in, or in other words, that the end of the face is not nearer the left foot than the heel.

The next most powerful club, meaning the distance which it will drive the ball, is the cleek.

This is an almost straight-faced iron club, and with it one should be able to get within about twenty or thirty yards of the distance one can get with a brassey. It is played practically like a brassey, and should be used in its place when one is afraid of overplaying with the latter, or when the lie is particularly bad and it is necessary to get distance.

Next to the cleek in power is the mid-iron, and then the mashie.

APPROACHING

Technically, of course, every shot, except the drive from the tee, which is expected to land the ball upon the green, is an approach, but the term is usually regarded to mean only shots played with a mid-iron or mashie, or, in other words, those from a distance of about 110 yards down to where the putter is employed. There are many ways of playing approach shots, and there is no more important part of the game than this, not even excepting putting, which is, I must confess, usually regarded as the most difficult and most important part of the game. While

TOP OF MID-IRON SHOT.

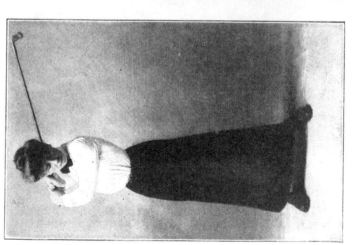

FINISH OF MID-IRON SHOT.

putting is undoubtedly of the greatest importance, the player who can lay her ball within a very few feet of the hole from a long approach shot practically saves a stroke, for she should occasionally go down in one putt, and always in two, while it is a grand putter indeed who can always go down in two putts when her ball lies thirty or forty feet away.

In playing approach shots, the importance of accuracy is intensified, for the distance to be covered is so small that the short player is just as well off as the long one, and the advantage which the latter enjoys from her superiority in that department from the tee and through the field is lost.

In playing a full shot, while it is extremely pleasant to see the ball go sailing away clean and sweet and dead on the line of the flag, it makes really no difference whether it does just that or whether it goes ten or fifteen yards to the right or left. When it comes to approaching the green, however, it is a different matter, and this ten or fifteen yards to one side or the other resolves itself into the question of a stroke more or less.

In playing approaches, the point mentioned in a former chapter regarding the use of a club which will carry the required distance without either pressing or trying to spare the shot is particularly apropos.

There are two ways of playing approach shots.

One is to play them up in the air with a little cut on the ball so that they will drop with comparatively little roll, and the other is to play them low and depend upon a long run.

Both have advantages, and while it is better to settle upon one way and use it whenever practicable, one should endeavor to master both methods, for upon every course there will be some holes where each will be found necessary.

When golf was younger in America than it is to-day, and our courses were consequently more imperfect and rougher, the highly lofted

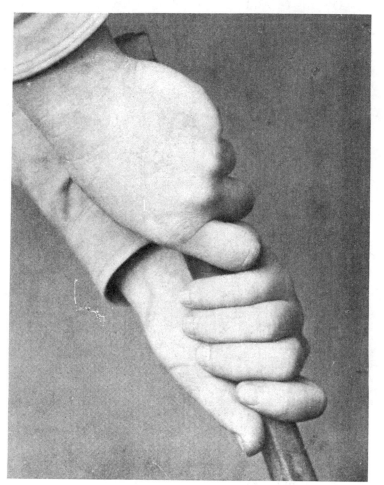

THE GRIP FOR IRON CLUBS.

approach which would drop with comparatively little roll was the favorite among players generally, from the fact that if one dropped the ball upon the green it ran truly, while an approach played so that it would bound and roll along the ground (which in those days was usually quite rough) exposed it to the chances of being turned widely from its true course by contact with the lumps in the ground.

A point against the highly lofted approach was that it was quite as liable to be swerved from its proper course by the wind as the low shot was by the rough ground.

This objection still holds good, while in the last year or two courses have improved so greatly that the ball in the vast majority of instances may be depended upon to roll straight, and for this reason the low approach shot is more generally used, when the conditions are such that a choice can be made.

Another point in favor of this style of approach shot is that it is decidedly easier to correctly gauge the proper amount of force necessary to cover a given distance when hitting with a straighter-faced club than when using a well-lofted one.

Still another point in its favor is that if one fails to hit the ball exactly as one should, the results are not so disastrous, for a half-topped or a sclaffed shot from off a comparatively straight-faced club gets much nearer the mark than when this unhappy result is achieved with a greatly lofted one.

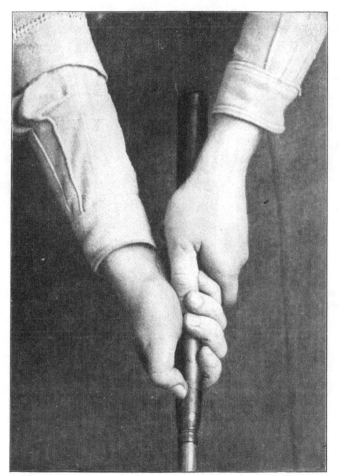

GRIP FOR APPROACHING.

CHAPTER VIII

ALTHOUGH the term " approaching " technically includes every stroke which will place the ball on the putting-green, be it made with driver, cleek, mashie, or even putter, the usually accepted definition of an approach shot is one made with a mid-iron or mashie, and executed with a three-quarters, one-half, or wrist stroke.

This is the first reference which I have made in these chapters to anything less than a full shot, and lest someone should mistake my meaning when reference is made to three-quarters or half shots, I will explain immediately that this is the manner in which shots executed with a swing which is but three-quarters or one-half of the arc described by a full stroke, are designated, and have no reference whatever to the distance about to be covered. Frequently a half-shot made by a person with especially strong wrists can be made to go nearly as far as a full shot.

The wrist shot is, as its name implies, made practically through the action of the wrists alone, and necessarily calls for the utmost accuracy and delicacy.

At the beginning of this work the point was made that it is much easier to play correctly a shot which would cover the distance with ease than to play it with a club with which one must press, and important as that point is in the playing of full shots, it is even more so when approaches are to be made. To my mind, the shorter the shot, the more difficult it is to play correctly.

In the first place there is always an instinctive feeling of carelessness induced by the apparent easiness of the shot, and this is the forerunner of a sclaff or a top.

In a short approach, too, these sins are

TOP OF SWING FOR 35-YARD APPROACH.

FINISH OF SWING FOR 35-YARD APPROACH.

usually more severely punished than the same deflections from the perfect stroke would be in a full shot. There is so little force behind a thirty- or forty-yard approach shot, that unless it is hit cleanly it will be considerably short, while if an amount of force is put into it sufficient to allow for a sclaff or top, and still reach the cup, then, if one happens to make the stroke cleanly, the ball will be away over the hole. In a full shot, on the other hand, the momentum of the club is so great that one can frequently sclaff a little or even half top the ball and still get practically the same distance as though it had been hit clean, and there is also the point that two or three yards, when one is one hundred and fifty yards away, make vastly less difference than does the same distance when one is thirty or forty yards away.

To emphasize the importance of good approach play would be futile. As one mentally reviews past matches and remembers how the medal at such and such a tournament was lost by a poor drive, it would seem as though the long game was by all odds the most important part of a successful career on the links. But at many another meeting we remember that the cup was lost despite a long game in which not even the most carping critic could find a flaw, and solely because of a poor approach shot now and then. Then it is that one forgets the fact that the long game is important and sighs, " Oh, for an always perfect approach! " And then again it is a great, albeit sad, truth that it is useless to hope to win golf matches if one cannot be sure of putting out in two after reaching the green.

So it goes. And the most important part of golf remains, like the will-o'-the-wisp, a phantasma which one wearily pursues only to find that, just as it is within one's grasp, it has changed its hue and the chase must be resumed once more. Still, good approaching means many saved strokes.

The player who can depend upon holing

out in three from the approaching distance
will never be beaten very badly.

The idea is of course to lay the approach
so close to the hole that one's first putt is
sure to be stone-dead, if not down indeed.
She who can do this should be happy.

Of course it is by no means impossible to
get down in two from whatever part of the
putting-green the approach has left you, but
it is an unpleasant feeling to reel at each
green that one must lay a thirty-foot putt
stone-dead, and even the best of us sometimes fail by a yard or two. Then, it is a
case of nerves truly.

No doubt all readers of this humble work
would be quite equal to holing eighteen
two-yard putts in a round, but everyone is
still mortal, and it is much better fun, to my
mind, to be three inches away and have one's
opponent playing to hole a two-yard putt for a
half than to be in that position one's self. Besides a stroke is a stroke, and one saved by
holing out in one putt is as valuable an aid to

winning a match or a medal as one gained in any other way. Decidedly, then, we must admit that approaching is useful.

Another point is that everyone holes a certain proportion of all putts, no matter what the distance.

And that proportion decreases very rapidly with each foot added to the distance to be holed.

It may be eighty or ninety per cent. at a foot, and it is quite likely to be one-tenth of one per cent. at thirty feet, and so naturally the more putts one has to hole at the shorter distance, the higher will be the percentage, and the greater will be the number of strokes saved.

In the last chapter I devoted considerable space to a discussion as to the advisability of playing one's approaches high in the air or running them along the ground, and therefore will pass over that point now.

When the distance is such that the player determines to make her approach with a cleek

TOP OF SWING FOR 80-YARD APPROACH.

FINISH OF SWING FOR 80-YARD APPROACH.

or iron, the stance and swing differ but little from those with which she has become familiar in learning to drive, except that one usually advances the right foot an inch or two more, and stands a little more upright, or, in other words, closer to the ball. Another point of difference is that the club should not go back so far in the upward swing, and it should also be raised more vertically, not trailed along back as closely to the ground as possible, as in a drive, and the difference should be accentuated as the distance of the shot decreases.

For making an approach shot of any distance between that for which a cleek is the proper club and approximately down to 100 yards from the hole, I use a mid-iron. In playing a shot of this kind, the same rules which governed the cleek play may remain in force, except that, as the distance to be covered in the shot decreases, the right foot should be advanced a trifle. The ball should also be a trifle nearer the right foot, say an inch or possibly two, than for a cleek shot.

The grip to be employed when grasping the club for a cleek or mid-iron shot differs slightly from that used when making a drive or brassey. As the accompanying illustrations show, the fingers grip the club somewhat more closely, the most noticeable difference being that the forefinger of the right hand is more closely wrapped around the club. After waggling and swinging the club backward and forward a few times to accustom one's self to the new way of holding the club, grip it tightly and take the proper stance. In doing this, it should be remembered that a straight line drawn through the center of the ball and the hole is the direction to be played for, and this must be aimed at regardless of where it seems from the stance that the ball should fly.

Also be sure that the face of the club, as its sole rests on the ground when addressing the ball, is at right angles to the line of play.

In making a drive, brassey, or cleek shot, it is an extremely desirable thing to hit the

ball with such cleanness that the ground remains untouched, but in making an approach
with a mid-iron, mashie, or jigger, the club
should be allowed to cut the turf a little, just
as the ball is struck by the club head and starts
away.   To allow the club to touch the ground
before reaching the ball would spoil the whole
stroke, as the ball could not then be hit clean,
and this is absolutely essential if a truly gauged
approach is to be made.   The club should not
be stopped in its swing, however, for as much
importance attaches to the follow-through of
an approach shot as to that of a drive.

CHAPTER IX

THE SHORT GAME (*continued*)

WITH the very agreeable supposition fixed in mind, if not in actual practice, that the cleek and iron have been thoroughly mastered, and that a shot of one hundred yards or more is now one of the easiest things in the world for her Ladyship-o'the-Links to accomplish perfectly, let us take up the shots which range from that distance downward until the putting-green itself is reached.

These may be played with a jigger, which is a sort of cross between a mid-iron and mashie, or a mashie itself, as the individual preference of the player may indicate.

In any event I adopt a decidedly different style of grip for playing these shots. As the accompanying illustration will show, my hands are interlocked as they are in the grip for driver and brassey, and in this particular there is little change. The radical point of difference lies in the position of the thumbs, and particularly the right thumb. This I press firmly on the top of the club shaft, so that my entire thumb is in contact with it. The advantage of this departure from the other grip is in the better direction one can secure with it when making a short shot.

When one is about to play an approach shot of one hundred yards or less, and there is no bunker or other hazard, the question arises whether to play a running-up approach or a boldly lofted one.

There are advantages to be gained from each style of play.

Providing it has been determined to play the lofted shot, one should take several preliminary swings a couple of feet away from the ball to gauge the force with which to swing in order to put the ball on the green. In the cleek and wooden-club shots, where one hits with only a desire to carry as great a distance as possible, a preliminary swing is useful only as a means of loosening one's swing, but in approaching it also acts as a gauge to the amount of force.

One of the greatest evils of a short approach shot is the tendency to drag the club through the stroke, as it were, instead of striking it sharply and firmly, as should be done. And the tendency to do this increases in the same ratio as the distance to be covered diminishes, for it seems, with but a thirty- or forty-yard shot to make, that if one hit the ball sharply it would go over the green.

The remedy for this is, of course, to shorten the swing until at some distances the club head may not swing backward over six or eight inches, while the entire action is brought about by the wrist alone.

As the right foot is advanced a trifle, when making a cleek-shot, over the position it should hold when making a full shot with a wooden club, so does the same foot con-

BEGINNING OF CUTTING UNDER-STROKE.

FINISH OF CUTTING UNDER-STROKE.

tinue to advance as the distance to be covered decreases, and the result is that when the player is making a thirty-yard approach, the right foot is so far in advance that its heel would be about two or three inches over a line drawn at right angles from the ball to the left toe. In the same ratio does the amount of space from the ball to the right foot diminish, so that when the stance for a thirty-yard approach is taken, the ball is within an inch or two of a line drawn straight through the heel and toe of the right foot, and perhaps from eighteen to twenty-four inches in front of the right toe. The instinctive effect of the advancement of the right foot has been to turn the body to the left—or towards the line of play, in other words—and in consequence one is practically facing the disk when making a very short shot.

In the performance of the strokes heretofore discussed, stress was laid on the importance of getting the weight and momentum of the body into them, but this becomes of less and less importance as the distance decreases. In fact, all the shots of from sixty to thirty yards should be made with the arms alone, although the body may be allowed to turn an inch or so if one feels that by so doing the swing will be freer. Under no circumstances, however, should one endeavor to have the body take any part in the stroke.

The action of the wrists is extremely important in all shots, and never more so than in approaching. In fact, when making shots of the shorter distance mentioned above, and under, one should use them to the very fullest extent, and hold the arms as immovable as possible.

The methods detailed above are those which are the natural results of the methods of making a full shot, modified to suit the conditions of the distance to be covered, and the system, I think, is certainly the best for that reason, if no other.

Still, one can make good approaches by keeping the elbows and wrists stiff and performing the whole stroke with the shoulders. The only advantage I can see to this style of play, however, is that the ball does not rise so high as it does when played in the other way—an advantage, it must be admitted, when the wind is blowing strongly; but this can be secured also by using a straighter-faced club with the other style of swing.

If you glance at the photographs illustrating the approach shots, it will be noticed that the knees are bent slightly more than they are when playing the long game, and that the body is likewise bent over a trifle more.

The weight of the body should be very gradually shifted from being divided pretty equally between the two feet, as it is in the long game, to the right foot as it advances with the shortening of the shot, but under no circumstances should either foot be allowed to move.

When playing a lofted approach, it is, of course, desirable to have as little run follow the landing of the ball as possible, it being thus easier to judge the distance to be covered.

After one has achieved a fair degree of skill, the ball, even if played naturally, will not run many yards. But still it may be wise to endeavor to acquire the art of playing short approaches sixty yards or less with what is technically known as a " back spin," the idea being to drop the ball dead. This comes into play most handily in such a situation as a green with a bunker or other hazard immediately at its back and something directly before it, over which the ball must be pitched.

There are not, it is true, very many such holes on the standard golf-courses, but time and again a match has been won or lost by a single hole.

The way to impart this back spin to a ball is to play it with a slice or cut, and this is made by drawing the arms in towards the body as they descend in the downward swing, stopping the stroke as soon as the club touches the ball. It is an extremely hard shot to play correctly, and I do not advocate it except in some extreme case like that mentioned above.

If one has a beautiful lie with the ball teed up so that it is easy to cut under it, the shot is not so impossible, but when the lie is bad, it is a " class " player indeed who can bring it off successfully.

If it is to be attempted, however, one must bear in mind that the effect of the back spin will be to make whatever run there is to the ball take effect to the right of the spot where it touches the ground.

This, of course, makes it necessary to play for the left of, and not straight at, the flag. Just how much allowance must be made, experience only can accurately tell, but it will be found to be somewhere around one or two yards. This shot should never be attempted when at a longer distance from the hole than sixty yards, for if it is, it is likely to be so greatly deflected that the result would be more disastrous than if played straight.

Nor is it good generalship to try to put a back spin on the ball because the wind is behind it. If the wind is strong the effect of the back spin will be neutralized, and if it is not strong, it will have but little effect on the ball anyway.

It is a fact that the longer an approach is, the less run there will be on the ball, and therefore a little twenty-five-yard wrist shot often has a longer run than a hundred-yard full iron.

Perhaps the best way to play a ball without run is to lay back the face of the club. When this is done the player should stand more behind the ball—that is, her left foot should be nearer it than the right. The same result may be accomplished by having a special club for just such shots made with

OFF THE RIGHT FOOT. FRONT VIEW.

OFF THE RIGHT FOOT.

OFF THE LEFT FOOT. FRONT VIEW.

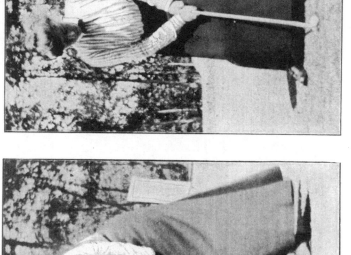

OFF THE LEFT FOOT. SIDE VIEW.

POSITIONS IN PUTTING.

the face abnormally laid back, but both of these methods are open to the disadvantage that with them the chances are about equal of cutting under the ball without touching it, and thus making a rank foozle.

CHAPTER X

APPROACHING AND PUTTING

THE very best way of all of playing an approach shot so that it will have a minimum of run after it lands is, like the best of everything else, the most difficult to acquire.

Among golfers it is known as "cutting the feet from it," and difficult as it is to put into execution, it is still more difficult to describe it so that an unpractical golfer will know what is meant. The accompanying illustrations, however, show the main point of difference from the ordinary approach shot very clearly.

The main point is the decidedly more perpendicular swing necessary for the stroke. The grip and stance need not be changed. The club must be brought down sharply and carried right into the turf, not swept over

140

it as in an ordinary approach shot, and then at the moment of impact the arms should be whipped right up into the air as quickly and as straight as possible, the whole stroke giving a decided snap to the ball. As it is necessary to cut well into the turf to perform this stroke with the best results, it should not be attempted unless the turf is soft enough to admit of a club cutting into it easily.

And while speaking of cutting into turf, in this connection I am going to give a bit of advice which will, I am afraid, bring down upon me the wrath of all Green Committees, but which I must perforce brave, if I am to set forth truly my ideas on the game.

In making all approach shots, I cut away the grass, and sometimes take a bit of turf as well, and I think that so doing adds considerable steadiness to one's play.

I am far from being an advocate of taking a divot with the stroke. There is nothing more reprehensible to my mind than the golfer who goes serenely along the course, tearing out great chunks of earth three or four inches long and equally wide, and from one to three inches deep, at each stroke. The class of golfers who do this are invariably not only of very mediocre ability, but they are either so ignorant of the rules and etiquette of the game, or so utterly selfish and careless, that they pay no heed as to where the divots fall or to the place whence they were torn. These become, of course, little cups into which the ball of the next player and all succeeding ones roll with unvarying regularity, with the result that it is rarely indeed that the ball can be played as it should be, and a loss of a stroke is thereby recorded.

No matter how small an amount of grass or turf be cut away, see yourself that it is replaced and trampled down. Far too many players leave this important duty to caddies, who, as a general rule, are carelessness and inefficiency personified.

Before closing the chapter on approaching, it is only right that the second most general method of approaching should receive mention. Of course every golfer will modify any style to a greater or less degree to correspond to her own personal likings and limitations, after she has attained a fair degree of proficiency, but next to the method already described, the majority of approaches are played from the stance technically known as " playing off the left leg."

In this position the ball is nearly on a line with the center of the left foot, and that is quite a distance back of the right one. The weight, instead of being principally on the right leg, is principally on the left, and the body is bent over a trifle more, perhaps, than in the other method. The arms also are kept in rather more towards the body.

I cannot see that there are any advantages in this method myself, but its advocates claim that with it one can secure a much straighter line of play, and when one is a little off in the orthodox method, it might be well to try this.

PUTTING

When the ball has once been safely landed
on the putting-green and mashie laid aside,
one lays aside with it all the pretensions to
a single style of play which has been under-
lying all the strokes heretofore discussed. In
other words, while all drives, brassey-strokes,
cleeks, and even mashie-shots are performed
by strokes the principles of which are based
upon one general principle, however much
individual preferences may cause them to be
modified, putting is performed exactly as
each individual player sees fit. One way
seems quite as good as another. The whole
point is to get the ball in the hole in the
fewest possible number of strokes, and there
are as many different ways of standing and
as many different ways of hitting the ball as
there are players.

Another point in which putting departs
from the other departments of the game is
that no player even pretends to always putt

in the same way or even with the same club. Of course the change in clubs might be explained by the difference in the nature of the turf over which one was putting if the games were being played on different links, but one is quite as apt to see the change in putting take place two or three times during the progress of a championship match on an eighteen-hole course, as on different days on different links.

All good golf depends more or less upon having one's eye " right," but this is very much more true of putting than any other stroke in the game. It is no uncommon thing for a professional or even a high-class amateur to take his stance, swing a driver two or three times over an imaginary tee, then blindfold himself, have a caddie tee up a ball on the spot over which his club swung before, and then drive away practically as good a shot as he would have done had his eyes been open. No one could hole a two-or-three-foot putt with eyes blinded, however, no matter how many times he or she had previously holed the putt from a certain stance.

The reason of this is, of course, the absolute accuracy required to putt the ball over a piece of turf, filled as are even the very best of putting-greens with miniature inequalities, and have it going with sufficient velocity to reach the cup surely, but yet not so swiftly that it will not be caught and held by the lip of the cup.

This cup is so small (it is barely $2\frac{1}{2}$ inches in diameter) that unless the ball strikes absolutely the center of the back of it, it will roll around the rim and run out, a performance which is one of the most annoying and exasperating things in the whole catalogue of such things, and of which it sometimes seems that the entire game of golf is completely composed.

It is a very strange, yet a very true, fact that hardly one golfer in ten realizes the important part which putting plays in the

STANDING SQUARE. FRONT VIEW.

STANDING SQUARE. SIDE VIEW.

game of golf, from the fact that, if one has become a fair master of the mashie and mid-iron, one may play along for a half-dozen holes or so and never be called upon to play a putt of more than six or seven feet, and this distance at a casual glance seems so insignificant as compared to the distances to be covered with drives or irons that the unthinking player immediately decides that the longer shot is of the more importance. A moment's reflection, however, shows most emphatically that it is not.

A player of average ability should reach three-fourths of the putting-greens in the average course in two strokes, and the other one-fourth in three strokes. Now, on the other hand, there are no players, even of the very highest class, who hope to hole out after reaching the putting-green in less than an average of two strokes, and there are quite as many times when three will be necessary as there are when it will be necessary to take three strokes to reach the green itself.

As it is sad, but emphatically the fact, that a putt of two inches counts just as largely in one's score as a drive of 200 yards, it will be seen that the number of putts required in an average game will be quite as great as the number of strokes of all other kinds combined required to complete the round.

If more golfers realized this there would be much more practicing done on the putting-green than there is to-day.

As a matter of fact, I think it is quite safe to say that many players, even among those who practice driving and approaching most conscientiously, never think of taking a putter in their hands, except during the course of a match.   Among the first-rank players, however, the reverse is quite true.   The few moments' practice with the wooden clubs and long irons suffices them, and then they will put in an hour holing out putts of from eighteen inches back to the edge of the green.

There is a term often used in the newspapers and among golfers which frequently puzzles those whose knowledge of the Royal and Ancient game is perhaps more confined to " hitting the ball " than studying the fine points of the game. This term is " the orthodox two putts," and comes from the fact that in figuring a par or a bogey score the player is allowed two putts after reaching the putting-green, whether the ball is on its extreme edge or whether it is within a foot of the hole.

The reason for this is, that in figuring par or bogey play it is customary to figure that one should be able to lie dead to the hole, —or, in other words, so close to it that the next stroke will certainly put the ball in in one shot, leaving the other for the accomplishment of the few inches which remain to be covered.

There is no less chance of winning a stroke on the way to the putting-green than there is once the green has been reached, for most of the average players will reach it in two or three or four strokes, as the case may be, as well as the most expert, the difference being in the nearness one reaches to the hole; and whether one reaches the green in a drive and mashie, or drive and brassey, and whether one is ten feet from the cup or twenty makes very little difference if one can putt.

Good putting goes by streaks. On certain days one cannot miss holing every putt for ten feet down, and occasionally one from the extreme edge of the green, while putts of a yard or two which formerly have frozen his heart with terror at the mere thought of trying to hole them, have become like delightful old friends of whose kindness and regard one is always sure. Miss them? Never; and the happy golfer cries, "Eureka! I have discovered the secret! No more will I mentally weep and gnash my teeth at the missing of the putts. The world is mine! Hurrah!" On such glad, glorious days as these even the putts of between eighteen inches and three feet, which are ac-

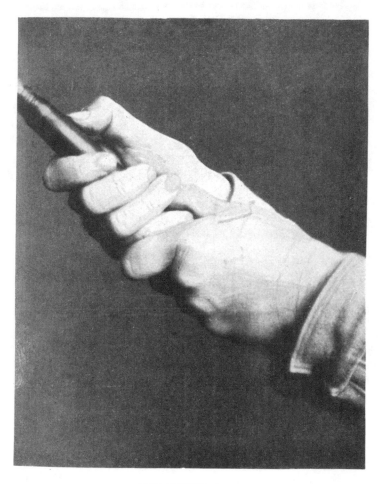

THE PUTTING GRIP.

knowledged by all players of quality to be the hardest to hole, lose their terrors.

To digress for a moment more: it is a fact, and a most curious one, too, that after a player attains a fair degree of proficiency, it is much harder for her to hole a putt of this length than it has been when she was much less expert in her general play.

It is a case of when too much knowledge is a dangerous thing, although not one of " where ignorance is bliss 'twere folly to be wise."

The reason for this apparent anomaly is that in holing a putt of a yard or less there is no particular credit. Everyone expects you to do it. You expect to do it, and you know everyone else expects so, too. It really looks so very easy, and in the early days of one's apprenticeship it would be, because one would go out with serene confidence that it would be impossible to miss it. After one has become something of a golfer, however, a long line of sad experiences which go to prove that it is quite possible, nay, even probable, that one will miss it, takes away this bland and cheerful confidence; and as one reflects on the putt, the resultant laughter which will follow if one misses, and the anger which will fill one's own mind, one becomes nervous, and unless one takes one's courage in hand at once and plays the putt boldly, disaster is sure to follow.

CHAPTER XI

NEXT to having one's eye " right,"
the most essential thing for successful putting is confidence, and
this is the explanation of the high average
that one can score when out on a green, practicing alone; so much higher, alas! than the
best one can do in a regular match or competition of any kind.

The fact that there will be dire conse-
quences ensuing if the putt is missed has a
most nerve-wrecking effect, and the more a
player ponders over the shot, the more nervous she will become. However, I do not
by any means advocate hasty or careless
putting.

One of the truest and best-known axioms

of the game owes its origin to the putting-green, and it is, " Never up, never in."

This is absolutely true, for, while the ball may go to the cup, it can never come to the ball. Consequently the first principle to implant firmly in one's mind when one reaches the green is always to be " up," or, in other words, always play the stroke strongly enough to run past the hole, if the ball does not go in. It is really surprising how fast a ball may be traveling and yet be caught by the rim of the cup, if it strikes it directly in the center; and playing boldly for the back of the cup is one of the never-failing distinctive earmarks of the " class " golfer.

When the putt to be negotiated is a yard or less long, one should hit the ball with sufficient force to send it about six inches to a foot past the cup, while from a longer distance one should play to overrun from two feet to a yard.

The advantages of this policy are many. In the first place, you will hit the ball with more confidence the harder you strike it, and, as I said above, confidence holes quite as many putts in a round as does skill. Then, again, a ball rolling swiftly is much less likely to be deflected from a true course by rough places in the turf than is one which is going slowly, and the hard-hit putt consequently goes down many times, when the gently tapped ball would be turned to one side by a bit of earth or a spear of wire-grass, and perhaps rim the cup.

Besides all these points, there is a glow of satisfaction which steals over one as the ball is heard banging against the back of the cup and dropping down with a thud. The feeling is not only an extremely satisfying one at the moment, but induces an accession of confidence at the next shot, and many more thereafter. And this is worth a good bit in a hard-fought match.

With all the above facts and fancies regarding the theory of putting inculcated, the next thing to do is to try to make the shot.

There are two prime essentials in the putting stroke,—one the grip, and the other the stance. To take up the former, the accompanying illustration shows clearly what I have found to be the best method. The club should be held firmly, but not so tightly that the muscles are rigid, and it may be held at either extreme of the leather on the handle, or at any intermediate place. Just as it is a wise plan to change the putting stance and the club itself when one finds that everything is not going as well as it ought, so it is a good plan to change occasionally the spot where one grasps the club.

There are three ways in which one may stand to negotiate putts, and each in turn deserves recognition. The first is standing with the main portion of the weight on the left foot; the next, with the greater amount on the right foot; and the third, with the weight resting equally between the two feet.

When the first method is used, the ball is placed nearer the left foot, and inversely when the second is employed, it is nearer the right.

With the grip and stance satisfactorily arranged, the next problem is how to hit the ball so that it will go into the hole. The first thing to consider is whether or not the lay of the ground between the ball and the cup is such that it would roll in, if it were hit with absolute accuracy. If this were usually so, putting would be robbed of half its terrors. Unfortunately, such is not the case. There are few putting-greens over which one does not have to calculate more or less for the undulation of the ground, and here is where some of the finest headwork called out in the entire game is displayed. Many players go to the opposite side of the hole from that at which the ball is lying and study its line from there, supplementing this scrutiny by another observation from the back of the ball, along the line to the hole. I believe, except in exceptional circumstances, that this is quite sufficient, and that trying to study the line from the other side only confuses one, and thus destroys the advantage already gained.

In calculating a putt, where it is necessary to allow for anything except the force and straightness with which one hits the ball, the best plan, I have found, is to take a small piece of grass or something similar, play directly for that, and trust that the lay of the ground will send the ball down into the cup.

In all putting, and particularly in such instances, judgment plays an important part. Little things, like remembering to play a putt on a rolling hill-side so that if the cup is missed the ball will stop on the downward instead of the upward side, from which it is, of course, easier to hole; using a putting-cleek with a loft to it instead of a straight-faced putter when the green is particularly fast; and there are a dozen other similar *nuances* serving to distinguish the good player from the bad one.

One of the most prominent is the question of playing for the hole or for a half, and many a match has been won or lost by good or bad judgment here. If one has only one stroke for a half, then by all means take any chance to hole the ball. For if the chance comes off, you are saved, and if not, you are lost anyhow. But when one has one to win or two to halve, and the match not at a desperate score, it is much better to get a sure half than try wildly to win, and end by not even getting a half. All that can be done is to point out similar instances, and leave the actualities to the player herself. And in speaking of judgment, the quality and nature of the greens to be played over are quite as important factors in deciding whether or not to change the putter as is the fact that one is putting badly.

On a really smooth and true green, with any keenness at all, the regular putter is quite as good a club as any, although many players prefer a putting-cleek under any and all circumstances. The advantage of it lies in the fact that it has a slight loft, and as this loft imparts a little back spin or cut to the ball, it can be hit harder, with less chance of over-running the hole, than if it were struck with the ordinary straight-faced putter. No matter what the club head may be, however, one should see that the shaft is stiff, as it is therefore much easier to gauge the amount of force required.

Wooden putters I consider distinctly inferior to metal, both from the fact that one cannot hit so hard with them, and greater delicacy of touch is therefore necessary, and from the fact that a ball is more liable to be deflected from its course off one of them than it is from a metal club. But some players use them with good effect for what are really short approach shots.

Putting, after all, is really a question of hitting the ball with the club face absolutely at a right angle to the hole, for if the ball strikes the back of the cup directly in the

center, it will stop and go in, even if running
with a pretty fair speed, and it is for this
reason that one sees good players always
rest the club for a second in front of the ball
before putting, it being, of course, easier to
get a line, without the ball to interfere with
the line of vision.

Of course, the old injunction of "keep
your eye on the ball" still holds its important position in the categories of golf, and
likewise the injunction not to move the head.
The body, also, for the first time should be
held immovable, for, in putting, the whole
stroke should be made with the arms and
wrists, and principally the latter. Still they
should not be allowed to predominate so
greatly that there is anything like a jolt in
the striking of the ball.

It should be a distinct hit, not a shove, but
the club should follow through after the ball,
and on a straight line along the line of the
putt desired. The elbows should be held in
well to the sides, as this makes it easier for

the club to follow through straight.   The
eyes should be fastened at a point just a fraction of an inch back of the center of the ball,
and great care taken not to look up for at
least a second after the ball has been struck
by the putter, and it is really remarkable
what a difference in one's putting this last
point makes.   In putting, I think a vast
majority of players have a tendency to
slightly pull the ball, just as in driving, the
majority have a tendency toward a slice; and
if one finds such is the case, try to hold the
left elbow closer to the side.

STYMIES

So much for putting when there are only
the ordinary troubles of ground and space
to overcome.   It is hard enough, even then,
to put the ball into the cup; but when to these
difficulties is added what is known as a stymie
the problem becomes difficult indeed.   A
stymie is that condition when the balls on
the putting-green are directly in the line of

play and more than six inches from each other.

There are three ways of getting your ball into the hole under these circumstances. One is to loft your ball over the other in a straight line; the second to roll it along the ground, and put a bias on it so that it will curve to one side of the other, go around the obstruction, and into the hole; thirdly, by striking the offending ball hard enough to knock it out of the way, and let yours follow on and go down.

Lofting the stymie is the more common way out of the difficulty, and the club with which to attempt it is a mashie, and the one with the most loft of any you own. The shot must be made entirely with the wrists, and the club cut under the ball without touching the turf. It is one of the most difficult of all shots, but as stymies must be played in all match-play tournaments, it is well worth cultivating.

The curve putt is made by turning the

face of the putter considerably to either the right or left, according as to which side the curve is desired, and hitting the ball so that the club is either drawn in or forced out, as the case may be, thus producing the desired " English " and its consequent curve.

TOURNAMENTS

No better fun, to my mind, can be imagined than playing in a tournament, whether it be a " picked-up " affair, arranged in five minutes, with a half-dozen starters, or a national event, which has been planned about and thought about for months, nor is there anything which will be of more benefit to one's game than participation in tournament play.

It gives a zest to the match which a man perhaps may enjoy by wagering his opponent on the number of strokes or holes he will be up or down, but which a woman can obtain only in this way, and it also has a steadying effect on nerves.

After playing in a few tournaments, the feeling of nervousness, which is bound to come to the most stout-hearted players in their first close match, wears away, and nothing more is thought of it.

The " gallery," as the crowd which follows the more important matches in big tournaments is called, is apt to have a very demoralizing effect on the player unaccustomed to spectators, but this is soon forgotten.

I do not believe that a woman should subject herself to any especial preparation for a tournament, except to get plenty of rest and sufficient practice in the two or three weeks before the tournament, so as to be at the top of her game. Such practice should consist of the usual routine, but should never, under any circumstances, be continued up to the very day of the tournament. Even if you should feel that you are in woeful need of practice, it is best not to touch a club for at least two days before the tournament. The reason for this is that if you play each day up to the beginning of the tournament, by about the twentieth or thirtieth day of it you have become overgolfed, and this means certain defeat.

One should always endeavor to play in practice against a stronger player, for in this way one becomes accustomed to being " down " throughout the match and outdriven from the tee. Consequently if one meets these conditions in a match, it is accepted as a matter of course, while if accustomed to being always the leader, it has a demoralizing effect to play someone who is as good as or better than one's self.

Tournaments in America are almost invariably arranged to begin with an eighteen-hole (or, for men, sometimes a thirty-six hole) qualifying round at medal or stroke play, the makers of the best eight or sixteen or thirty-two scores, as the case may be, continuing on at match or hole play.

This is, all in all, the best way to conduct

a tourney, I think, for it not only gives a chance to as many as wish to compete, but it makes it necessary for a player to be adept at both medal and match play. There are many old-fashioned persons who maintain that only match play is golf, and that it is the only form of the game which should be considered, but I do not agree with them. No one can be considered a really high-class golfer who cannot play well at either form of the game.

In tournaments it is popularly supposed that the players are drawn by chance to play as partners on the qualifying round, but the Goddess of Fortune usually receives a little aid from the tournament committee in making her selections. This is quite as it should be, for the entry list contains players of every imaginable amount of ability, and to force a first-class player to play with a fourth-rank enthusiast, who has entered in hopes of a miracle happening, is manifestly unjust to both,—to the best player, because the poor play of her partner makes her play carelessly, and a little sympathetically, as it were, while the poorer player, after a few holes, becomes demoralized at the superior play of her partner, and " presses " in a vain attempt to hold the same pace, with the consequence that she returns a score several strokes worse than it should be.

The question of whether or not the draw for the match play should be " arranged " or left solely to chance has many good arguments on either side. Those who advocate that it should be left to chance point to the fact that sometimes one player will have a series of desperates matches to reach the final round, while the other contestant will have a very easy time. A case in point is the national championship tournament of 1899, when Mrs. Caleb Fox, the runner-up, in order to reach the finals, had to meet Miss Beatrix Hoyt (the title-holder), Miss Marion Oliver, and Miss Anna Sands, playing extra-hole matches with the two latter, while Miss Underhill, the ultimate champion, had a very easy time reaching the final.

Another argument against the " arranging " of the draw is that there are no two women in America, who stand so pre-eminent that it would be fair to put them at opposite ends of the draw, and give them as easy a path as possible to the finals. Such being the case, it seems to me that the partners for the qualifying round should be selected so as to give each person as equal a partner as possible, but that in the match play chance should decide the drawings.

In a tournament I believe that the best way to do is not to try and defeat your opponents by an overwhelming score, or to strain every effort to leading the field in the qualifying round, but to play along with the greatest ease consistent with winning the match or qualifying. In this way, when the crucial test comes, you will be able to play at your very best, whereas, if one has exhausted one's energies in breaking records and endeavoring to win by 10 up and 8 to play in eighteen holes in previous days, this will be impossible.

To be a successful tournament-player, no matter how skillful one may be, it is essential to be able to use the occasion, and " play better than one knows how," as the sporting papers say when the occasion demands it. Women, I am proud to say, show a relatively greater degree of nerve in golf than do men, and particularly is this so when on the putting-green.

CHAPTER XII

HAZARDS AND GENERAL REMARKS

IN the instructions which I have given in the foregoing chapters I have written upon the supposition that the ball is lying upon the fair green and not in any hazard. The definition of the latter is, to quote from the rules of the United States Golf Association, " Any bunker, water (except casual water), sand path, road, railway, whin, bush rushes, rabbit scrape, fence, or ditch. Sand blown in the grass, or sprinkled in the course for the preservation, bare patches, snow and ice are not hazards. Permanent grass within a hazard shall not be considered part of the hazard."

It will thus be seen that playing from a hazard carries so many conditions that ability to play out of one with the loss of but a stroke at most, or perhaps without any loss at all, is a most valuable acquisition to one's game. As if the adverse natural conditions existing in a hazard were not enough to handicap the player the rules of the game provide that nothing in a hazard—such as a loose piece of dead wood, a stone, or anything which interferes with the performance of the stroke, and which, when existing on the fair green, can be moved—can be touched.

In other words, no matter how bad the lie, the ball must be played as it is found.

And the point which adds difficulty to the playing out of a hazard is that the rules prohibit the soling of one's club, the great advantages of which one does not realize until one is deprived of the benefit of so doing. It gives a steadiness to the stroke, an assurance to one's swing, and, above all, a confidence which is worth a great deal. The most important consideration, when one finds the ball in a hazard, is to get it out.

Of course if you can play it on the green,

or if it is a hazard a long distance from the cup, get a shot of considerable length on the line to the hole, so much the better, but if this is impossible to do, be satisfied to get well out. It is much better to get well out, playing the ball in a directly opposite direction to the hole, than to play it straight for the hole and run a risk of not getting out. This applies only, of course, as a general thing. There are cases when it is do or die, and then every chance must be risked.

As an instance, suppose you are in a bunker before a hole and playing 2 more than your opponent, who is on the green, and practically sure to go down in 2 more.

Your only chance is to get on the green from the bunker, and trust that you can get down in another, so that your opponent will miss her putt and give you a half.

If playing medal play it would probably be better to play back, and surely get on in the next, than to run the risk of not getting over, for by that time you would have played so many more that the hole would surely be lost. That is, supposing you are playing match play.

An alternative to either playing back or directly from the hole is to play over at an angle.

If, however, there are reasons,—such as hazards on either side, or whatsoever it may be,—that cause you to decide not to try and play off at an angle, and you are going to play back, be sure that you go back far enough.

It makes no difference whether you have to play a mashie-shot of ten or of twenty-five yards; and if you hit at the ball with a determination to go the latter distance, you are pretty sure, even if you foozle, to go the former, while a foozle from a shot meant for the lesser distance will probably fail to get out of the hazard.

It is also well to remember this point if the green is a long way off, for if one plays back far enough to use a driver or brassey instead of a mashie, the extra distance the wooden club will give will more than make up for the extra distance back one must play in order to be sure of clearing the bunker with it.

Playing from a bunker requires a very different sort of stroke than does playing a ball lying in the fair green.

For a bunker shot it is not desirable to hit the ball cleanly, as it is when in the fair green. On the contrary, the point is to hit behind it and cut through the sand.

In playing a bunker shot it is usually difficult to get a firm stance, for the soft sand gives under your feet as the weight of the body swings over to the right, no matter how firmly one may think one is standing. It is well, therefore, after obtaining the stance wanted, to work one's feet into the sand, and get as near the foundation of the bunker as possible. It is also advisable to place the feet a little further apart than usual if one can feel natural and at ease when so doing, but if not, then use the regular stance.

Grip the club firmly with both hands, for the stroke to be made is one of brute force. All finesse and delicacy of touch are forgotten. One must "club" the ball, and the more vertical the swing the better.

It is because of this that many men who have been baseball players, and then taken up golf, play this sort of shot better proportionately than they do any other, for the swing is just like the one they learned when playing baseball.

As it is the object to hit the sand behind the ball and not the ball itself, the eye should be fixed on a point an inch or two behind the ball.

It is a good idea to hold the club for a second directly over this spot, being very careful not to let it touch the ground, and then swing it back as straight up as possible. In learning to play bunker shots, the natural tendency will be found to hit too near the ball, if not the ball itself, for the one great point which the learner has been trying to observe is to hit the ball, and therefore she will instinctively keep on trying to do so. Therefore it is better to try to strike the ground a couple of inches back of where one really wishes the club to come in contact with it, in order to allow for the instinctive and at first uncontrollable tendency to hit the ball.

All the above points apply to bunker shots when there is a cop two or three or more feet high within a yard or so of the ball. When it is lying in a trap bunker, as are called those which are merely shallow sand pits without cups around them, a rounded swing, more like that used for a fair-green shot, may be used. One may also return to the original principle of hitting the ball instead of back of it, except that it is well to sclaff a little. When the ball is in long grass the same principles should be employed as when it is in a bunker,—that is, the straightest possible swing should be used, and the ground struck a few inches back of the ball instead of the ball itself. The reason for this is that if the rounder and longer swing is used, the grass is apt to catch it and break its force, and even if the force is not broken, to deflect it from its course. Another point to remember for use in an emergency, both when playing from a hazard, and at any other time, is that by turning the face of the club the ball can be made to fly at an angle, even when played with a straight swing, and this knowledge is often handy when there are trees or fences or other obstructions which make it impossible to play a full stroke in the direction in which it is wished to send the ball.

Another point which most beginners seem to find impossible to comprehend is that the loft which its maker gave to a mashie or niblick is quite sufficient to loft the ball when it is struck with the ordinary stroke. Why this is such a difficult matter to understand I cannot imagine, but it is a fact that nine out of every ten players make the mistake. That it is one, a moment's reflection will show, for if the club's face were not made as it is for just this purpose, why should it be changed from the straight face of a cleek?

Under no circumstances, therefore, try to make a swing which will aid the ball to rise —all that you need to do is to play the stroke correctly and see that you hit the ball.

Of course if you are within a couple of feet of the high bunker, and it is surely a case of "lost hole," unless you clear it, it is advisable to turn the club in your hand so as to lay back its face a little, and to stand a little further behind the ball than usual, but under ordinary circumstances the club's face will do all that is required, provided you hit the ball squarely

CADDIES

The question of a caddie is a serious proposition, and it bears a very prominent relation to one's game. This is true of masculine golfers as well as feminine, in a measure, but its importance is much greater with the latter than with the former.

The reason for this is merely a question of temperament. Men by all the laws of nature and science are much more independent and self-reliant than women, and consequently they are much less apt to be influenced by the actions of their caddies.

The duties of the caddie, to quote from the formal language of the United States Golf Association rulings, are simply to carry one's clubs; but besides this he may give advice.

There has been considerable discussion aroused at the National Women's Golf championship of the past two or three years over the question of caddies, but it seems to have worked out its own salvation. The argument first started over the fact that a number of the contestants in the tournament had excellent amateur golfers to carry their clubs and act as advisers. This was all very well for those who had plenty of friends at their call who could play good golf, but not every contestant was in so fortunate a position, and some of those who were not tried to equalize matters by hiring professionals.

I can see no reason why this was not quite as fair as it was to have a first-class amateur act in that capacity, for, while the professional might be a little better player, he would be no better coach and have no better judgment than the amateur. As a matter of fact, he, in all probability, would not have the ability to inspire anything like the steadiness and confidence which the amateur, from his superior intelligence, would, and so would not be so useful at a most essential part of the duties of a caddie. Very few of the players seemed to realize this, however, and some rather severe criticism has been hurled at those who have had professionals to carry their clubs in tournaments. The chief accusation seems to be that it was taking an unfair advantage. This it might be were only one player to do so, but when more than half of the chief contestants are doing it, I must confess I cannot acknowledge the justice of the insinuation. If everyone would agree to abolish every kind of caddie except the regulation small boy, who is merely useful as a means of propelling one's bag of clubs over the links, well and good, but until there is some such agreement, I think the matter is one of individual choice, and all players should be left to decide the point for themselves. Precedent certainly indorses the employment of professionals, or anyone else whom the player wishes.

There has never been a question raised in America as to a man's using a professional if he so desired, and it has been done very frequently. Why, therefore, it should be considered unfair or unsportsmanlike for a woman to have her clubs carried by the best caddie she can obtain I cannot understand. Not only in tournaments, but in general play, does the caddie play an important part. If he is a good one he is of much service, but I would much rather, and I think that nearly all players will agree with me, play a round with no caddie at all in preference to having a poor one.   There really are no good caddies in this country except professionals. The average caddie on an American course is a boy ranging from ten to sixteen years of age, who looks upon the carrying of clubs as an irksome means of making money, and a thing which must be shirked as much as the good nature or ignorance of the player for whom he is carrying will permit.   He knows nothing of the game.   He is unable to tell you whether the distance of any shot is such that you should use a mashie or a driver, and, above all, he never knows how many strokes your opponent or even you yourself have played.

He insists upon lagging about ten yards behind you, and annoys you not only by his indifference in this respect, but never under any circumstances handing you the club necessary for the shot, even if you tell him yourself which one you want.

The simplest part of his duty, building your tees, he cannot do properly; and if you are foolish enough to try to have him do it, he will either build you a miniature mountain of sand, or else put down such a tiny pinch that you will be forced to sclaff badly in order to hit the ball at all.   As for finding your ball after a shot, the average caddie never thinks of such a thing.   If you are fortunate enough to have driven it straight down the fair green, where it is in plain sight, this negligence of his will not prove costly, but if a slice or pull or a bad bound has sent it off the course into long grass, or any other place where it will be difficult to see readily, the caddie will be the most absolutely helpless and ignorant person as to its whereabouts of anyone on the entire links.   I have never had the pleasure of playing golf across the ocean, but from what I hear, the caddies over there are the exact opposite of the boys who make life for the American golfer a round of misery.   There the caddies begin to carry clubs when they are as young as our American caddies, but, unlike them, they do not give it up at the end of a year or two. On the contrary, many of them have spent their entire lives carrying golf clubs, and they know every inch of the distance and every spear of grass on the courses. They know even better than you, perhaps, what club you should use for each and every shot, and they are as keenly interested in your play and as jubilant over a good score as you ever could be yourself. A lost ball with one of these old Scotch caddies is an almost unheard-of occurrence, while I do not suppose there was ever one known to annoy his employer by lagging behind during the round. How to obtain a class of caddies of this caliber is one of the great problems of American golf, and until it is solved the game will lack the very highest acme of enjoyment.

Conditions might be very much improved if the professional of each club would hold a sort of school for fifteen or twenty minutes each morning as soon as the caddies reach the clubhouse. He could explain to them just what their duties were, what they should do, and how they should do it, and if every club would adopt this idea, there is no doubt but that the caddie service would soon reach a much higher plane than it has at present.

BALLS

The evolution of the golf-ball has been rapid and radical in its development. For a great many years golf-balls were made by taking a round leather cover and stuffing it full of feathers, pounding them down so that several quarts of feathers were compressed into a globe about an inch and a quarter in diameter.

After using this kind of ball for years and years, someone discovered that gutta-percha would make a much more lively and much more durable ball than the one of compressed feathers; and although its introduction was bitterly opposed by the best players of the time, its qualities were so superior that it quickly won its way, and for a long period of time was the standard ball. There were a great many makes, and they were made with different varieties of "nicks," and all were about equal in desirability and excellence.

No one thought that there could ever be an improvement made upon the gutta-percha ball, but during the last three years Yankee genius has invented one which is as much superior to the "gutty" as the "gutty" was to the old feather ball. It is made by taking a rubber core, and winding it with a thread of pure rubber until it is very nearly the size required. (The regulation ball is of 27½ pattern, but there are some used 27 size and a few 28.) After the thread of rubber, tightly stretched across, has been wound around the rubber core (the process being done by machinery, of course, to secure absolute mechanical accuracy), the ball is incased in a thin shell of gutta. This shell is not more than about one-sixteenth of an inch thick, as its only object is to furnish a surface upon which the nicks, necessary in order to obtain the greatest flight to the ball, can be made. Another consideration is that it may save the rubber thread from being cut by a stroke of the club, and by the stones on the course. The difference between this ball and the regulation " gutty " is, of course, in its resiliency.

Experts who have used both balls differ as to whether they can get a longer one from a driver by using a " gutty " or the new rubber-filled ball, but all agree that one can obtain from ten to twenty-five yards farther with the new kind from an iron-shot. For the mediocre player there is no doubt that the new ball is a distinct advantage. She can drive it much farther, whether she is using a wooden or an iron club; it will roll nearly as far after a topped shot as though it had been struck truly; and, best of all, it has a happy faculty of bounding along the

MISS RHONA K. ADAIR, *PUTTING*.

ground and jumping over the bunkers, which rejoices exceedingly the heart of a player who is accustomed to spending a large portion of her time in sorrow and sadness, striving to play the aggravating ball from the hazard. It is not, however, so pleasurable a ball to use as the " gutty," if one is playing a fairly good game, for a cleanly hit full shot from the latter gives a click, as the ball and club come in contact, which is the sweetest of music to a golfer; on the other hand, the rubber-filled ball flies off the club with a soft, squashy sound, as though one had hit a lump of putty. Still, it requires much less effort to drive it than does the " gutty," and as endurance plays a considerable part in golf matches, this is a strong point in its favor.

No matter how much cut is put on a high approach shot, it is impossible to make the rubber-filled ball drop dead, and on some greens it is almost impossible to play it without running away past the hole. However,

its advantages much more than counterbalance its disadvantages to my mind, and particularly so for women. All golf-balls should
be kept for some time before being used, the
" gutty " ball from eight or nine months to
a year, and the rubber-filled ball a little less,
and all balls, no matter what kind, are improved by being remade. This can be done
by any golf-club maker, or molds can be
bought for a few dollars in which a player
can remake the balls herself. Sometimes the
paint will chip off when the ball has been kept
for a long time, but this may be remedied by
dipping the ball in fairly hot water for a little
while, in order to moisten up the paint. Care
should be taken not to allow the ball to become soft by staying in the hot water too
long, however, and in summer, during the extremely hot weather, it is a good idea to keep
one's golf balls in as cool a place as may be
convenient.

After a ball has been used for a
little while, the most satisfactory thing to do

and the most economical as well, is to send it to a professional or to one of the big ball-making manufactories, and have it remade. Any ball manufactory will do it for one dollar to two dollars a dozen, or they will exchange old balls for new ones. If, however, one delights in trying to do things for one's self, a can of paint prepared especially for renewing the whiteness of golf-balls may be purchased at any golf-goods store, and the player can re-paint them herself. The ball should first be soaked in a solution of potash or lye until the old paint has been entirely removed. Let them dry for a day or so, and then they can be painted, either with a brush or by taking some paint on the palm of one's hands and rolling the ball around in them. About four coats of paint will be required, and I think that one experience at trying to become a golf-ball maker will be all that anyone will require to satisfy herself that this is a department of the game better left to those who make a business of it.

COURTESY

The etiquette of golf suggests many little points of courtesy which any player of experience would, from instinctive good breeding, recognize, but there are some little points which, through carelessness, are not always observed, and it would add much to the enjoyment of those playing on the same links, and detract nothing from their own pleasure, if their attention should be called to them. Of course any woman playing in a match whose opponent lost her ball, would, from innate courtesy, try to help her find it, and likewise, no one would think of leaving the tee, having had the honor, before her opponent had played, nor would anyone think, no matter how careless she might be, of moving or speaking while her opponent was preparing or making her shot.

All these and many more matter-of-course courtesies are extended from one opponent to another, but there are some courtesies due to the players directly behind one, and also directly preceding one, which are frequently not accorded, and it is to these that I wish to call attention.

If you are playing in a match, in which your opponent is a very slow player, or if you are one yourself, or if, for any reason whatsoever, you find that you are falling behind the player just preceding you, and are, in consequence, delaying all those behind you, it is only the courteous thing to allow the player behind to pass. So annoying and disastrous to good play is it to all those behind that I really think a rule should be framed providing that any player playing so slowly as to compel the player behind to wait, should be compelled to give way, and let the fastest players go on.

As conditions are now, few players like to request permission to pass a player ahead of them, no matter how slowly the former is proceeding, and many players are offended at such a request, thinking, most unnecessarily and unjustly, that such a request is almost in the light of an insult, or at least a reflection on their playing ability. Such is by no means the case. It is simply a recognition of the fact that some people naturally play faster than others, and if by the luck of the start a slow player begins her round early, she should be considerate enough to allow anyone who plays faster to pass her.

If the conditions are reversed, and you and your partner are the faster players, you would naturally appreciate such courtesy, but, on the other hand, you should remember the feelings of those in front of you. The rules of the game provide that a player must not play a shot until the players preceding have played their second, but, unfortunately, this rule is very frequently forgotten, or at least over-looked.

CORRECTING FAULTS

No matter how good a player may be, there will inevitably come a time when she will get off with some club or another, and for a certain time will be absolutely unable to make a shot with it. The very best way to regain one's skill, when this unfortunate state of affairs happens, is to take a complete rest and not touch any club for several days, or, if one feels that it is necessary to play, endeavor not to use this particular club. If a little rest does not put one back in form, take a dozen old balls, and practice that one particular shot for half an hour. In this way one will generally be able to discover what is wrong, and this is not only the best way to practice to obtain skill, but it is by all means the best way of correcting faults.

CHAPTER XIII

GOLF COURSES FOR WOMEN

GOLF in America has spread to such an astounding degree in the comparatively few years of its existence that the links over which it is played are laid out on any and all sorts of ground. In Scotland and England the great majority of courses are laid out on flat sandy ground, and one does not have to use up the best part of one's strength in the physical exertion of climbing up and down hill. Owing to the varying characteristics of country in the United States, however, many popular links are laid out, from necessity, on ground which is so much up and down hill that a woman is really tired out from the exertion of walking before half the course is played. Even for a man, it is decidedly unpleasant to play over hilly links.

For a woman it makes the sport so arduous that it is only the most intense enthusiast who will play very steadily or for a very long time. In choosing, therefore, land on which to lay out a golf links, the first consideration, in my opinion, is to select ground over which it will be easy to walk.

The ideal soil on which to lay out a golf course consists of a sandy subsoil, with a quick, thickly growing turf, a turf which will give at the impact of a club and which will grow again very quickly. This is the kind of soil which is found in almost every instance in England and Scotland, and it is only on account of the recuperative powers of the turf there that permits of the really wonderful amount of play which goes on all over the foreign links. In this country Garden City approximates more nearly the ideal turf than does any other links, but the Chicago Golf Club at Wheaton, the Apawamis, Nassau, Morris County, Baltrusol, Glenview, and Midlothian Clubs also have splendid turf.

To my mind, turf is a secondary consideration to a level or slightly rolling country, and I should, therefore, place it in the secondary point of consideration when fixing upon a site for a course.

For the really scientific and high-class playing of the game of golf it is absolutely essential that the distances and hazards of the course be so arranged that every good shot is rewarded and every poor one penalized. Unfortunately, there are very few courses in America on which this is invariably the rule at each hole, although the number of properly laid out links is increasing every day. To a certain extent the rubber-filled ball which has come into prominence and popularity within the last year or two is responsible for this state of affairs, for playing with it, anyone gets a longer shot, and this is particularly emphasized in the case of a woman. Consequently a hole which, when laid out to be two full shots with a wooden club, playing with the old gutta-percha ball, becomes, when played with the new one, a drive and iron shot, which, of course, is a bad hole, for the reason that if the drive is a bad one, one can still reach the green by using a driver or brassey for the second shot, instead of the iron, and thus be exactly as well off at the end of the two shots as though the first one had been played perfectly and the second played with an iron. It is this sort of thing which breaks a good player's heart. She says to herself, " What is the advantage of my making a drive forty yards further than my opponent, if the latter can be on the green in two, just as well off as I am, even though she may have used a driver, while I played with a mashie." In laying out a course, therefore, the first thing to be considered is that each hole should be one, or two, or three, or four, as the case may be, full shots from tee to green. In considering what distance a full shot should be counted one must endeavor to strike the distance which a first-class player averages to drive. For a woman, 160 or 170 yards is a fair distance, and for a man 20 or

30 yards may be added to that. In determining the distances of the holes, however, the natural lay of the land must be taken into consideration and, as in everything else, an arbitrary rule must give way to common sense. For instance, if the line of play is over a slight down grade one can count on ten or fifteen yards' roll for the ball, while if it is over a slight up-grade a similar distance must be subtracted from the number determined upon as the average full shot to counterbalance the fact that there would be little less flight and much less roll than if a shot were played on an absolutely level piece of ground.

HAZARDS

The distances of the holes, however, are not the only requisites for the laying of a first-class golf links. The proper placing of the various hazards which lend a spice and variety to the performance of the shots play a very important part in the construction of a scientific course. In the first place, there should never be a hazard placed so as to endanger a good shot, let alone trap a phenomenally good one. This would seem to be the most ordinary of common sense, but I have frequently seen bunkers and hazards so placed that the exceptionally long player was worse off than the short driver. The fundamental principle of arranging the hazards is to punish every poor shot without placing any good shot in jeopardy, and if this principle is kept firmly in mind there will be comparatively little trouble in arranging the course properly. A hazard does not need to be formidable to have all the effect which is its purpose. The moral effect of a hazard is usually quite as great if it is a bunker three feet high as if it is ten, and as the moral effect is quite as important as the material difficulty to be surmounted, the smaller one is consequently quite as useful as the other.

In my opinion it is not necessary or even advisable to have hazards on a course from which it is extremely difficult to get out.

I think that one shot lost is quite penalty enough in medal play, and, as for match play, if one can't win the hole after receiving the advantage of a stroke, then one deserves to lose it. In my tournament experience I have seen so many first-class players fail to qualify in a medal play round simply because one bad shot landed them in a hazard so difficult that it required six or eight strokes to get out on the fair green again, and their chances for the entire tournament or championship were lost just through this one bad stroke. It was a misfortune of this kind which caused Miss Frances Griscom, then the title-holder, to fail to qualify in the Woman's National Championship of 1901, and many other nearly as notable instances will be recalled by anyone who has followed the tournament play of American women during the past few years. Not only should bunkers be made small enough, so that a really good player can get out in one stroke, but they should be turfed over, and then a rule made that the ball should

be played from where it lay, and not dropped
back a club's length. Another point is that
for at least five or six feet back of the bunker,
in the direction from which the shot is to be
played, the turf should be taken up and the
hole filled in with soft sand, in order that one
can cut deeply under and behind the ball, and
thus get over the bunker, a thing which is
practically impossible when the soil is hard or
turfed.

The following table of distances should, in
my opinion, form an almost ideal course for
women's play, although, of course, the nature
of the ground might cause some alterations to
be necessary:

1.—365 yards, driver, brassey, mashie, 2
    putts.
2.—340 yards, driver, brassey, 2 putts.
3.—179 yards, driver, 2 putts.
4.—395 yards, driver, brassey, half-iron, 2
    putts.
5.—320 yards, driver, mid-iron, 2 putts.

6.—465 yards, driver, brassey, mid-iron, 2 putts.

7.—280 yards, driver, half-iron, 2 putts.

8.—375 yards, driver, brassey, mashie, 2 putts.

9.—400 yards, driver, brassey, mashie, 2 putts.

10.—167 yards, cleek, 2 putts.

11.—335 yards, driver, cleek, 2 putts.

12.—300 yards, driver, mid-iron, 2 putts.

13.—378 yards, driver, brassey, mashie, 2 putts.

14.—350 yards, driver, brassey, 2 putts.

15.—180 yards, driver, 2 putts.

16.—425 yards, driver, brassey, mashie, 2 putts.

17.—387 yards, driver, brassey, mashie, 2 putts.

18.—343 yards, driver, brassey, 2 putts.

Total, 5984 yards.　Bogie, 77.

IMPRESSIONS OF AMERICAN GOLF

BY MISS RHONA K. ADAIR

I AM afraid that this is a pretty big subject to write about, for, to tell the truth, my individual impressions are not quite so keen as they might have been had they not been fogged a bit by the wave of pleasure and all-round jollity into which I was plunged almost the moment I put foot on the steamship dock.

Perhaps the best starting point is by a compliment which I can pay with the utmost sincerity to the American woman golfer. It is one equally deserved by Mrs. Charles T. Stout (who is, I consider, decidedly the best American woman player I have seen), and by the poorest player that has been at any of the courses over which I have played.

This is in regard to their pluck. Never in

all my experience have I seen such universal grit, sand, or what I believe you call " nerve " as is displayed by every woman golfer in America. It is really astounding. I don't believe that there is a bad sportswoman in America. Certainly, if there be one, I have not seen her. In England it is very uncommon to find a woman playing out a hole if she has been bunkered, or was driven out of bounds, or is for any reason whatsoever playing several strokes more than her opponent. I find in America, that with the never-say-die spirit which I have always heard was typical of all America, they keep right on playing until their opponent's ball is actually in the hole. Nor does this apply to one hole only of a match. I have seen women with a score of four down and five to go staring them in the face tee up with quite as much pluck and cheerfulness as they showed on the first tee, and in a good many instances with much more. That is the spirit which wins golf matches, and while I am loyal to the last to my home and friends, I must in fairness admit that American women seem better able to rise to a bad situation and play " better than they know how " when such a feat is demanded by the exigencies of the score, than either English, Irish, or Scotch women.

It may be that I have been particularly fortunate in the friends whom I have made in America and in the atmosphere into which I have been drawn at the tournaments I have attended. But it seems to me that there is a much greater degree of good-fellowship and sociability connected with your meetings than there is on the other side. During a match there it is quite as unusual for opposing players to chat during the round as it seems to be unusual here for them not to do so, and in this way one, of course, gets much better acquainted than is possible when a round is made in silence, except for the formal courtesies and speeches of the game. Then, too, over here girls become better friends in a week's tournament than they would in England in two or three such meetings, and this, it seems to me, is one of the most charming features of American tournaments.

A point which seems most curious to me is the difference shown in dress when golfing by American women. At home we wear about the same things whether the weather is pleasant or unpleasant. Over here, it seems to me, the girls pay rather more attention to their clothes and general " get-up " when the sun is shining than we ever do. But they also go to the other extreme, and when the weather is unpleasant they simply do not care what they wear.

In England, dowdy and careless in dress as we are supposed to be, I have never seen women in such unbecoming and careless and rough costumes as I have seen here. So far as the nature of dress for play is concerned, I think we all dress about alike. A heavy pair of boots, any kind of a short skirt, and a waist which leaves one free for a good full swing are all that are necessary, and they

are alike the world over. It is more common
for women to wear gloves on the other side
than it is here, I think, and that little detail
is simply another link in the chain of plucki-
ness of which I spoke above, the inference
being that the American woman would rather
take the trouble to massage and manicure out
the grime which she is bound to accumulate
without gloves than to run the risk of spoiling
a shot by a glove slipping in her grasp. So
far as clubs are concerned, I don't see any appreciable difference in those made here and
those made on the other side, although perhaps we at home use a slightly lighter club
than the average woman here. After all,
though, a good club's a good club, and must
be suited to its owner and no one else.

Of the American courses I have nothing
but praise. They far exceed what I had been
led to expect, and while improvements could
be suggested, one or two at which I have
played rank quite on a par with the best links
abroad.

Of course the nature of the soil is different, and so are the turf and putting-greens, but the latter average to run quite as true as ours at home, although they are not, as a general thing, so large. I think that the average of putting should be better here than in England, for the reason that your greens are much slower than ours, and the slower the green the harder one can hit the ball.

I have been simply astounded at the excellence of links which I have been told were only three or four years old, for we believe that a course must have been played over several years more than that number to reach its greatest perfection. Should some of the links I have seen improve in the next few years as much as they have in the past, they will be the best in the world.

American men may have an advantage over our masculine players through using a rubber-filled ball, but our women have adopted it almost altogether, and I think that its use not only improves one's game, but adds a deal of enjoyment to playing, as with it one is not compelled to exert anything like so much strength to achieve the same results.

This is a valuable point in any country, but particularly so in the United States, where I find that the climatic conditions are such that physique plays a very important part in one's golf. I think it is no exaggeration to say that it takes more strength to play an eighteen-hole round in the United States than to play thirty-six holes at home, and this is due solely to the atmospheric pressure and not to any appreciable difference in the lie of the land.

Despite this fact, however, I do not think that there is much difference in the length of carry one obtains from a shot, the ball flying to all practical purposes as well here as at home.

It is because of the fact that thirty-six holes of tournament play are too much to ask of a woman in America in one day that I think that the qualifying round, as you play it here, is a decidedly necessary adjunct to tournaments. I thoroughly believe that match play is the truest golf, and hope that at home we shall always decide our tournaments by it exclusively; but with the big fields which you turn out here, one of three things must be done in the decision of tournaments. Either there must be two rounds of eighteen-hole matches each day; tournaments must last two weeks, or there must be a qualifying round, and this last is, by all odds, the best alternative.

There are, of course, other arguments in favor of the qualifying round aside from the one of time-saving.

In the first place, it teaches carefulness and steadiness, and steadiness is what the American player lacks more than any one other thing. Match play, with all its advantages, does induce a degree of carelessness in play when one feels that a hole is hopeless from the fact that one says, " Oh, well, one hole—what does it matter?" while in medal play, with every stroke counting, a moment's carelessness may mean loss of the medal or tournament.

One great fault, which it seems to me is very prevalent in America, is in the fact that American women devote too much time to perfecting themselves in one stroke, and not enough to the all-round development of their game. I have found, in consequence, that the women here can average a much better drive than they can any other shot, for, as driving is the most pleasurable part of the game, they have developed their skill at that, without re-gard to iron-shots or putting.

American women really drive quite as well, if not better, than do English women, and, for this reason, I am convinced that the time is not far distant when the standard of skill will be as high on this side of the ocean as it is on the other. If a team of six or eight American women come abroad next year, as I hope they will, I expect our team to defeat them, but from what I have seen here we shall have to bring out our very best players and

have them at the very top of their game to do
so.

By all odds the best woman player in the
United States whom I have seen is Mrs.
Charles T. Stout. I consider her, all things
taken into consideration, a wonder, while
Miss Margaret Curtis is a phenomenal driver,
and at times an extremely brilliant player.
She is so erratic, however, that she cannot be considered as being in Mrs. Stout's
class.

In fact, Mrs. Stout, I have been told, was
considered by all good judges here to be quite
in a class by herself, and from what I have
seen I am quite prepared to accept their ver-
dict as being true. Never have I seen a player
display more ideal form than does she in every
particular, and, in my opinion, she is quite the
equal of any woman golfer in the world. Her
play is a worthy model for every woman to
pattern after, and, should she come abroad
next year for the Ladies' English championship, she would have a chance second to no

one's of winning it. Besides the beautiful style in which she plays, the main beauty of her game is that it is so evenly developed, and not one stroke perfected at the expense of others.

Of the American Amateur champion, Mr. Walter J. Travis, I can only express admiration. His game, while not as good relatively to that of our best amateurs, as is Mrs. Stout's to our best women's, is one which deserves the highest consideration in any company, and when I was told that he did not begin to play golf until several years past thirty, I was more than amazed.

I have seen very few other of the high-class amateurs play here, but from what I have heard of the way Mr. Travis outclasses them, I do not think that they rank so well relatively with our amateurs as do the women.

SHOT MOST NECESSARY

In considering such a point as this, it must not be overlooked that on any links, and under any circumstances, it is putting which wins the match.

In America, as I said above, it strikes me that women and men, too, pay far too much attention to driving, sacrificing everything to it, while at home, if any stroke is practiced to an undue proportion, it is putting. From the nature of the majority of the links over which I have played in America, I should say that ability to play a low, rolling-up approach shot would be as useful a shot as anyone could name. I had been told before my arrival that I would have to pitch up all my approach shots, and endeavor to have them drop dead, but I found that a running-up approach sufficed in most instances.

CADDIES

Really, the only thing in which I found America much behind us at home was the caddies.

Much as I hate to seem unpleasant or captious, I must say that I consider the genus caddie, as found on American links, the worst fraud ever perpetrated. They know nothing; they are lazy and indifferent, and it is almost as much trouble to make them keep up with one on the journey round the links as it is to caddie for one's self. Generally they do not know one club from another.

At home the caddies are usually men who have been born and brought up on the links, and are really almost as much use to a player as a professional is here. They are uniformly faithful and courteous.

The Last Hole

Hints to Golfers

By NIBLICK

Tall 12mo, Illustrated with Marginal Sketches and Diagrams

Net, $1.25

FOR SALE NOW AT ALL BOOKSTORES

WALTER J. TRAVIS, Amateur Champion U. S. A. for 1900–1901:
"It is undoubtedly the best book on golf which has yet appeared or will appear for many a day."

HARRY VARDON:
"Your book is one of the best in the market. It fills a long-felt want. Everything is nicely explained and the book ought to have a great sale."

H. S. C. EVERARD (St. Andrews, Scotland), Author of "Golf in Theory and Practice":
"I am certain I cannot vie with you in the elaborate detail in which you have discussed the scientific points of the game. This feature of your book fills me with astonishment. You have set forth in lucid style principles which many who have spent a lifetime over the game have not yet mastered, all showing the mastery you have attained of what is really a difficult subject."

WHO IS NIBLICK?

SEVERAL months ago this book was issued privately in Boston. The identity of "*Niblick*" has been and is a matter of constant speculation among golfers. Various professionals have been named as its author, but "*Niblick*" is still known only as the author of *the best book on Golf yet written*.

¶ It is now published through THE BAKER & TAYLOR Co. and may be bought at bookstores or directly from the publishers.

¶ Attractive illustrations, with little brownie golf balls on the margins, a striking binding and a well-ordered text and index make this book the standard in make-up as well as matter.

WHAT PROFESSIONAL GOLFERS SAY

TOM MORRIS (St. Andrews, Scotland)

"I have studied it all through, and find a great deal of useful information in it which should prove very beneficial to players. Of the different points mentioned, every one will be able to pick out something to his advantage."

JOSEPH FLOYD:

"The book explains golf in such a simple manner that any beginner car understand it. Other books on golf are so complicated that it is almost impossible to follow the instructions."

A. H. FENN:

"I have read the book with profit. It is the best book on golf I have seen, and I have made a study of golf the last seven years. If I could have ad it when I started teaching it would have saved me lots of hard work."

ROBERT STROMAR·

"It is without doubt the best book out on golf. All one has to do is to commit to memory the hints contained, and he will improve his game a third of a stroke."

JOHN HARLAND:

"'Hints to Golfers' furnishes excellent suggestions to the golfer, whether he be a novice or a scratchman. I recommend it highly and consider it a valuable addition to golf literature."

JAS. H. T. BROWN:

"The book explains the game of golf and how to play it so real that if all the golfing world perused it my profession would soon be a thing of the past."

DONALD J. ROSS:

"I have read it over carefully, and I feel sure that the expert golfer as well as the beginner will find it both interesting and instructive. Every golfer ought to read it."

JAMES N. MACKRELL:

"I must say that your hints are exceedingly valuable to golfers and the book ought to aid those who are in want of advice when they cannot readily get instruction from a professional."

JOHN JONES:

"My opinion is that beginners and golfers in general ought to add a copy to their library, as there are many useful hints in it which I think would help them to understand the professionals when teaching them."

THE BAKER & TAYLOR CO.

Publishers, 33-37 East Seventeenth Street, NEW YORK CITY

WITH THE TREES

An Opinion of the Day

From The Nation (New York), June 20, 1895

"In a modest preface Mr. Lee gives the formation of the United States Golf Association at the end of last year as the raison d'être of this manual. His main purpose in writing it was, doubtless, to record the constitution and by-laws of that association, and the conclusions arrived at by its officers in the important question of rules.... But Mr. Lee has gone considerably further than this, and has produced an attractive volume which contains all that is really essential to the beginner in the way of book-learning. In these days, when all the young men and maidens who are not learning to ride a wheel are struggling with the mysteries of golf, a brief account of the best methods of meeting the initial difficulties and of making the ordinary shots cannot fail of a warm welcome. Of course the tyro must not expect to drive 200 yards at once as a result of reading this or any other manual. In all probability he will never drive that distance except in his happiest dreams. But Mr. Lee's advice, if carefully combed over from time to time after a day's practice in the field, will inevitably improve his games."